The 800-Pound Gorilla. Limits to Group Structures and Asset Partitioning in Insolvency

The 800-Pound Gorilla. Limits to Group Structures and Asset Partitioning in Insolvency

Preadviezen / Reports 2018

Richard Squire, Joeri Vananroye, Arie Van Hoe, Gillis Lindemans, Arpi Karapetian, Frank M.J. Verstijlen and Aart Jonkers

eleven
international publishing

Published, sold and distributed by Eleven International Publishing
P.O. Box 85576
2508 CG The Hague
The Netherlands
Tel.: +31 70 33 070 33
Fax: +31 70 33 070 30
e-mail: sales@elevenpub.nl
www.elevenpub.com

Sold and distributed in USA and Canada
Independent Publishers Group
814 N. Franklin Street
Chicago, IL 60610
USA
Order Placement: (800) 888-4741
Fax: (312) 337-5985
orders@ipgbook.com
www.ipgbook.com

Eleven International Publishing is an imprint of Boom uitgevers Den Haag.

ISBN 978-94-6236-957-3
ISBN 978-94-6274-644-2 (E-book)

Table of Contents

Table of Contents

Limits to Group Structures and Asset Partitioning in Insolvency

In insolvency procedures, administrators have to accept the estate as they find it. Furthermore, administrators are commonly appointed in the proceeding as to a specific legal entity and have to respect the separate legal personality. By means of limited liability and separate legal personality, groups can incorporate in ways where liabilities and assets are allocated in different legal entities. This creates room for opportunism, especially in relation to creditors.

The 2018 NACIIL annual reports focus on the theme 'Limits to Group Structures and Asset Partitioning in Insolvency'. This theme encompasses two related topics at the intersection of corporate law and insolvency law: (1) the artificial subdivision of enterprises over different legal entities (asset partitioning) and (2) selective perforation by means of guarantees.

There are different manifestations of artificial subdivision of enterprises over different legal entities. The clearest and most blatant one is an artificial division within a group between profit making and loss making parts. Also, increasingly common are corporate structures where an operating company is insolvent, but cannot be sold to outside parties because the IP rights or other key assets required for running the business are held by another group company. Dutch law and other legal systems are struggling to come to terms with such cases of asset partitioning. Belgian law is more creative and has for example implemented rules requiring that in case of asset sales out of insolvency, the acquirer should also be able to make a bid on the necessary 'missing assets', thus protecting the value of a company in insolvency. Reports on the topic of asset partioning are prepared from a Dutch perspective by prof. F.M.J. Verstijlen and A. Karapetian, from a Belgium perspective by prof. J. Vananroye, A. van Hoe and G. Lindemans and from a U.S. perspective by prof. R. Squire.

The second topic deals with guarantees. After the division of a company into subsidiaries, the first step is often to selectively perforate the newly created limited liability structure in favor of financial creditors. The question could be asked whether, in such a selectively pierced group structure, the separateness of the legal entities the group consists of can and should still be taken seriously. Counterintuitively, in practice the legal rules applicable to group guarantees seem very friendly to financial creditors. The law for example often provides that guaranteed creditors can claim up to the full amount in the different proceedings. Although the impact of these rules on the pay out to other creditors is very strong, there is excessive attention for real security rights and only scant attention for the rules on guarantees. In the words of prof. W.H. Widen (US): "If secured lending presents fairness problems, the unsecured syndicated guarantee may be the 800-pound gorilla in the corner that goes unnoticed." The reports have been prepared from a Dutch perspective by A.L. Jonkers, from a Belgium perspective by prof. J. Vananroye, A. van Hoe and G. Lindemans and from a U.S. perspective by prof. R. Squire.

In short, enterprises can be constructed in many different ways, leading in practice to enterprises being separated into many different group companies. This opens the door for opportunistic practices which insolvency laws have to come to terms with. The NACIIL/NVRII board hopes and expects that the reports will provide a stimulus for the debate on the question to what extent insolvency law has to accept corporate structures as they have been designed or whether insolvency law should under certain circumstances take a more critical approach.

NACIIL/NVRII Board, 2019

Limits to Group Structures and Asset Partitioning in Insolvency: Suppressing Value and Selective Perforation by Means of Guarantees

NACIIL Annual Meeting, Amsterdam, November 15, 2018

*Richard Squire**

It is my pleasure to submit this final report in connection with our conference on November 15. I divide my comments into the two distinct but related topics of the conference: (1) suppressing value in insolvency by taking out key assets, and (2) selective perforation by means of guarantees. Limiting my comments to my area of expertise, I address solely American law, in particular U.S. bankruptcy law and creditor remedies under the laws of the various states (which are often enforceable in federal bankruptcy proceedings).

1 Suppressing Value in Insolvency by Taking Out Key Assets

When affiliated American business entities enter bankruptcy, they tend to so *en masse*. It is unusual for a parent or subsidiary corporation to enter bankruptcy alone; the failure of one member of a corporate family tends to pull down the others as well. This commonality of fate arises from both economic and legal ties. Economically, affiliated business entities tend to produce the same (or complementary) goods and services and thus rise or fall upon the same vagaries of supply and demand. Legally, the entities typically tie their fortunes even more closely together by investing in each other (through loans or equity positions), guaranteeing each other's outside debts, and inserting cross-default provisions in their loan agreements that make a default by one member an event of bankruptcy for all.

Legal ties in the form of intragroup guarantees and cross-default provisions influence the decisions of group managers. When one group member is teetering on the verge of failure, the managers have a strong incentive to shift assets into it, to prop it up. In this way, interconnected loan arrangements induce group managers to move assets into insolvent entities instead of taking assets out of them.

* Alpin J. Cameron Chair in Law, Fordham University School of Law.

Of course, what we might call "selective" bankruptcy – the strategic placing of a single group entity into bankruptcy, in an attempt to confine losses to its creditors alone – is not unknown in American legal and business practice. And once managers have decided that the best approach is to tie off a struggling member from the rest of the group, as if to limit hemorrhaging by application of a tourniquet, their incentive reverses: rather than moving value into the entity to shore it up, they may wish to strip it of as much value as possible, rescuing assets for the benefit of the group's shareholders while increasing losses for the doomed entity's creditors.

A vivid example of such conduct is provided by the January 2015 bankruptcy of Caesars Entertainment Operating Co. (CEOC) and the events leading up to it. This company was a member of a corporate group that owned casinos and other gambling-related assets, primarily in Las Vegas. An ill-timed leveraged buyout in 2008, consummated shortly before the worst days of the nation's financial crisis, burdened the group with debts it had no hope of repaying. Between 2010 and 2014, the group's managers effectively created a "good Caesars" and a "bad Caesars" by shifting assets out of CEOC, which bore much of the group's debt, and into affiliates. CEOC's creditors sued its parent entity in 2014, seeking to recover the value of the transferred assets. Shortly thereafter, CEOC filed for protection under Chapter 11 of the U.S. Bankruptcy Code, which contemplates reorganization of the debtor, as contrasted with liquidation.

Recognizing that the claims against the parent likely had merit, the bankruptcy judge ordered an examiner to appraise them. The examiner estimated that the estate's claims against the parent were worth between $3.6 billion and $5.1 billion. The examiner's report, submitted on March 15, 2016, is worth reading, as it describes well the primary mechanisms by which American law polices the stripping of assets from insolvent companies and illustrates their application to numerous types of transaction.[1]

In the end, the estate did not bring the claims, and the creditors' direct actions against the parent did not reach judgment. Instead, the parties compromised the claims through the reorganization process. Initially, the corporate parent (as controlling shareholder) proposed a plan under which the bankrupt subsidiary's junior creditors would recover approximately 9 cents for every dollar owed.[2] However, the stark findings of the examiner's report strengthened the creditors' bargaining position in the reorganization, and the final plan confirmed by the bankruptcy court in January 2017 provided payouts to junior creditors worth 66 cents on the dollar.[3] This hefty increase in recoveries was the result of the parent's agreement to pay money into the estate, revealing the potency of the creditor remedies available to combat strategic asset stripping of a corporate entity.

1 Final Report of Examiner, Richard J. Davis, In re: Caesars Entertainment Operating Co., Inc. (Bankr. E.D. Ill.) (March 15, 2016).

2 S. Indap, "Caesars Gets Confirmation for Bankruptcy Plan, Concluding Multi-Year Saga," *Financial Times* (January 17, 2017).

3 *Id.*

In the following discussion I will address the main legal mechanisms under U.S. law for policing strategic asset stripping of insolvent companies. The first three remedies mentioned (for constructive and actual fraudulent transfers and for breach of fiduciary duties) are the most powerful in cases involving large corporate entities with sophisticated legal representation. They are also the remedies the examiner in the Caesars case considered to be most valuable to the estate. The next two remedies (veil piercing and substantive consolidation) are likely to be useful in a smaller set of circumstances, for reasons that will be described. Finally, I address how lenders use the law of secured transactions, as well as simple contract law, to protect themselves against the "two-legged stool" maneuver, which while apparently a problem in certain Continental jurisdictions is rare in the United States.

1.1 Constructive Fraudulent Transfers

The law of fraudulent transfers (or, to use an older but still oft-heard term, fraudulent conveyances) has deep roots in Anglo-American law, originating in a statute enacted by the English parliament in 1571.[4] Modern versions of that statute can be found on the books of every U.S. state as well as in the U.S. bankruptcy code. As the term "fraudulent" indicates, these statutes originally targeted transactions in which debtors *intended* to harm their creditors. I discuss the law of such "actual" fraudulent transfers below. However, in the 20th century, amendments to the statutes widened their ambit to cover "constructive" fraudulent transfers – namely, transactions that objectively harmed creditors, irrespective of the debtor's intent. Today, creditors – and parties acting on their behalf, such as bankruptcy trustees – are more likely to seek relief under these constructive fraudulent-transfer provisions than to attempt to prove the debtor's ill intent. They are therefore the provisions under which creditors are most likely to obtain relief for the most common forms of debtor misconduct in corporate groups, such as asset stripping.

In bankruptcy, a trustee (or the debtor in possession, who normally acts in place of the trustee in a Chapter 11 proceeding) has two options for pursuing a fraudulent-transfer claim. First, the trustee can sue under the Bankruptcy Code's § 548, which comprises a federal version of a fraudulent-transfer statute.[5] Second, the trustee can avail himself of the option accorded by § 544 to seek relief that would otherwise be available to the debtor's creditors under state law.[6] Most U.S. states have enacted some version of the Uniform Fraudulent Transfers Act, whose substantive elements are the same as those of § 548. Therefore, the trustee will generally have to prove the same factual allegations under either approach. However, § 548 has a limited look-back period, permitting the

4 Fraudulent Conveyances Act 1571 (13 Eliz 1, c 5).
5 11 U.S.C. § 548.
6 11 U.S.C. § 544.

trustee to "avoid" (render null) transactions only if they occurred no more than two years before the bankruptcy filing.[7] State law often provides a longer look-back period, which the trustee may invoke via § 544.

To prove a constructive fraudulent transfer, the trustee must establish two elements. First, he must show that the debtor transferred an asset, or incurred an obligation, without receiving a "reasonably equivalent value" in exchange.[8] The Bankruptcy Code defines value for these purposes as "property, or satisfaction or securing of a present or antecedent debt of the debtor."[9] As this definition suggests, the statute contemplates a kind of balance-sheet test, asking whether the consideration for a transaction was sufficient to prevent deterioration of the firm's net asset value. However, some bankruptcy courts have weakened the protection of creditors by crediting debtors with various kinds of "indirect" value that seem not to satisfy the statutory definition of value. Typically, these consist of advantages to affiliated entities that may redound to the debtor's advantage, under the theory that the group members constitute a single business concern.[10] This loosening of the definition of value is vulnerable to criticism on grounds that it views benefits and costs from the perspective of the group's ultimate shareholders, whereas fraudulent-transfer law is instead meant to protect creditors.

To satisfy the second element of a constructive fraudulent-transfer claim, the trustee must prove that the transfer occurred under circumstances, specified in the statute, when harm to creditors was especially likely. There are different sets of circumstances that satisfy this element, and the trustee need only establish one. Most commonly, the trustee seeks to prove that the debtor was insolvent at the time of the challenged transaction (or made insolvent by it).[11] Courts normally define insolvency for these purposes as an excess of liabilities over assets, with assets measured at market value. The idea is that creditors are the residual claimants of an insolvent debtor and thus bear the cost of transactions that deplete its net assets. Alternatively, the trustee can prove that the debtor "was engaged in a business or transaction, or was about to engage in a business or transaction, for which property remaining with the debtor was an unreasonably small capital."[12] Since valuation is an imprecise science, this alternative permits the trustee to prevail even if he can show only that the debtor was on the knife's edge of insolvency when it gave away property or incurred new debt not matched by an infusion of assets.

If the trustee can establish both elements of a constructive fraudulent transfer, the challenged transaction is deemed void. If it is a debt or other obligation of the debtor, it is unenforceable in the bankruptcy proceeding, except to the extent the debtor is solvent.

---

7 11 U.S.C. § 548(a)(1).
8 11 U.S.C. § 548(a)(1)(B)(i).
9 11 U.S.C. § 548(d)(2)(A).
10 *See, e.g.,* Rubin *v.* Manufacturers Hanover Trust Co., 661 F.2d 979 (2d Cir. 1981).
11 11 U.S.C. § 548(a)(1)(B)(ii)(I).
12 11 U.S.C. § 548(a)(1)(B)(ii)(II).

If it is an asset transfer, the trustee may sue to recover on behalf of the estate the assets (or their value) from the transferee or from any party the transfer benefited.[13]

The Caesars bankruptcy report illustrates the power of these constructive fraudulent-transfer provisions to reverse transactions that deplete an insolvent entity. In 2011, when CEOC (the future debtor in bankruptcy) was insolvent by any conventional measure, it transferred to an affiliated entity (owned by the same corporate parent) the rights to host the World Series of Poker, a gaming and media event whose trademark it controlled. As ostensible payment, the parent reduced by $20.5 million a debt the subsidiary owed it on a revolving line of credit. The examiner estimated that the hosting rights were worth at least $50.3 million, indicating that the debtor did not receive a reasonably equivalent value in exchange for them. Therefore, the debtor should have been able to recover the hosting rights or their value, *i.e.*, $50.3 million.

If the transferee received the hosting rights in good faith, the statute would have granted it a lien on the debtor's estate to the extent of the value it provided, which here would arguably be the $20.5 million in forgiven debt.[14] But good faith would be difficult to prove on these facts, as the transferee was an affiliated entity under the control of the group's parent, whose managers would have known both that the transferring subsidiary was insolvent and that the price paid for the hosting rights was inadequate. Therefore, the debtor most likely would have been able to recover the hosting rights and also keep the $20.5 million credit received for them. In this way, constructive fraudulent-transfer law can have a strong deterrent effect, leaving group members who engage in asset stripping worse off than they would have been otherwise.

1.2 *Actual Fraudulent Transfers*

As an alternative to proving the two elements of a constructive fraudulent transfer, a bankruptcy trustee can nullify a transfer or obligation of the debtor by showing that the debtor committed an actual, or intentional, fraudulent transfer. Such a transfer occurs when the debtor acted with "actual intent to hinder, delay or defraud" any of its creditors.

To determine whether intent to harm creditors motivated a debtor, courts will typically look to "badges of fraud," which are objective indicators of subjective ill intent. Two of the traditional badges of fraud – insolvency at the time of the transaction and lack of fair consideration – now also form the basis of the law of constructive fraudulent transfers. But there are other badges that remain particular to actual fraudulent transfers, such as that the transaction's counterparty was an affiliated or controlling person, or that the transaction improved such a person's position in the debtor's bankruptcy.[15]

13 11 U.S.C. § 550(a).

14 11 U.S.C. § 550(c).

15 Final Report of Examiner, Richard J. Davis, 2016, p. 40.

Intent to harm creditors is hard to prove in most cases. If the debtor can identify a legitimate business reason for a transaction – a reason unrelated to harming creditors and plausibly likely to increase profits – then courts will often treat this as conclusive proof that the transaction was not an actual fraudulent transfer, the presence of badges of fraud notwithstanding. A more sophisticated approach has been taken by the United States Court of Appeals for the Seventh Circuit, which is based in Chicago and has jurisdiction over federal bankruptcy cases in Illinois, Indiana, and Wisconsin. This appellate court has instructed bankruptcy judges to find intent to harm creditors where such harm was a transaction's "natural consequence," even if the debtor can also identify a business purpose for the transaction.[16] This focus on consequences can be interpreted as establishing a presumption that debtors intended to cause harm to creditors if, when considering alternative means for achieving a legitimate business goal, they did not select the means least likely to cause such harm.

The Caesars case also provides an example of what the examiner considered an actual fraudulent transfer. In 2012, the corporate parent wished to refinance $4.5 billion in debt but lacked sufficient assets to do so at a serviceable interest rate. In other words, its equity value was too low to make it creditworthy. Therefore, in 2013, the parent transferred real estate worth approximately $350 million out of CEOC. No direct consideration was paid to CEOC, but the parent's senior creditors (who had sponsored its leveraged buyout) argued that CEOC would enjoy indirect benefits exceeding the value of the real estate transferred. The examiner rejected this valuation, finding that the transaction reduced CEOC's net value by approximately $250 million.[17]

The transfer bore several badges of fraud. CEOC was insolvent when it occurred, the consideration was grossly inadequate, and the transferee was owned by CEOC's parent. Moreover, the transfer improved the parent's position, at the expense of CEOC's creditors, in case of CEOC's bankruptcy, which was likely given its insolvency. In addition, the assumptions used in the valuation of CEOC's indirect benefits from the transaction were manifestly dubious. Finally, the parent engaged in self-dealing – it was on both sides of the transfer, controlling both the buyer and seller – yet it did not attempt to secure a price that was fair to the seller (CEOC), instead using a low price that harmed the seller's creditors. The examiner further opined that, as a result of this actual fraudulent transfer, CEOC should have been able to recover the full value of the properties it had relinquished.[18]

---

16 In re Sentinel Mgmt. Group, Inc., 728 F.3d 660 (7th Cir. 2013).

17 Final Report of Examiner, Richard J. Davis, 2016, pp. 44-46.

18 *Id.*, at 47.

1.3 *Breach of Fiduciary Duties*

A third avenue for relief in asset-stripping cases is the corporate law of fiduciary duties. A shareholder who controls a corporation owes fiduciary duties to the corporation and its minority shareholders. Normally, only the corporation, or one of its shareholders through a derivative suit, can bring an action against a fiduciary to enforce duties owed to the corporation. If, however, the corporation is insolvent, courts will permit its creditors, or a trustee acting on their behalf, to bring a fiduciary-duty claim.[19] The idea is that the creditors are then the residual claimants to the corporation's assets and thus have the proper incentive to represent the corporation's interests in derivative litigation.

When managers of a corporate group pull value out of one group member in anticipation of dropping it into bankruptcy, the value is typically transferred to the parent corporation or to a sibling subsidiary owned by the parent. For this reason, such transactions can usually be characterized as instances of self-dealing by the parent, whereby the parent enriches itself, or its affiliate, at the expense of the corporation it controls. Self-dealing by a fiduciary implicates the duty of loyalty, requiring the fiduciary to show that the transaction was entirely fair to the corporation and its shareholders. One important element of fairness is price. If a transaction was one-sided, so that the consideration received by the corporation was less than the value of what was taken from it, then the fiduciary may be guilty of a breach of duties and required to restore what has been removed or pay compensation.

Fiduciary-duty law seemingly has the potential to be a more effective device for recovering stripped assets than fraudulent-transfer law. As noted earlier, the typical fraudulent-transfer claim to reverse asset stripping requires proof not only that the debtor did not receive a reasonably equivalent value, but also that the debtor was insolvent or lacked adequate capital at the time of the transaction. A fiduciary-duty claim, by contrast, may require only the first showing – unfairness of price, which tracks the equivalent-value element. Insolvency, or lack of adequate capital, is not normally an element of the cause of action. Or, to put the matter another way, for creditors to sue a fiduciary for breach of duty, they must show that the corporation is insolvent when the action is brought, but they need not show that the corporation was insolvent at the time of the asset stripping. Insolvency is relevant to the plaintiff's standing; it is not an element of the underlying claim.

Unfortunately, this distinction is not always recognized in practice. For example, in his report on behalf of the Caesars estate, the examiner analyzed CEOC's potential fiduciary-duty claims by inquiring into CEOC's insolvency at the time of each value-draining transaction. He did this because he characterized corporate fiduciary duties as normally being owed only to the corporation and its shareholders, but expanding to embrace creditors when the corporation is insolvent. While this was once the standard way of con-

19 N. Am. Catholic Educ. Programming Found., Inc. *v.* Gheewalla, 930 A.2d 92 (Del. 2007).

ceptualizing the law of fiduciary duties vis-à-vis creditors, it is no longer the proper articulation of the law in Delaware, the leading jurisdiction for American corporate law. Under Delaware law, corporate fiduciary duties are never owed to creditors as such; creditors merely acquire the power to sue on behalf of the corporation to enforce those duties when the corporation is insolvent.[20]

There is, however, another reason to suspect that the solvency of the corporation at the time of the transaction may remain relevant, even under the Delaware Supreme Court's current conceptualization of fiduciary duties. As noted, the standard statement is that a fiduciary owes duties to the "corporation and its shareholders." At first blush, this statement seems redundant, for what is a corporation but a legal fiction created to serve the interests of its shareholders? By serving "the corporation," whose interests could a fiduciary advance if not those of shareholders? The older conception of the scope of the duties – expanding to embrace creditors when the corporation is insolvent – seemed to provide a conceptually satisfying answer to this question. But that answer has been foreclosed by the Delaware Supreme Court's insistence that fiduciary duties are never owed to creditors as such.

Perhaps the answer now is simply that the fiduciary must maintain the value of the corporation, irrespective of whether doing so advances shareholder interests or creditor interests. But this attempt to distinguish the corporation's interests from those of its shareholders presents its own difficulties, as it would seemingly make the payment of dividends impermissible. Therefore, to the extent that maintaining the value of the corporation is a duty distinct from the duty to advance shareholder interests, it can only be relevant under conditions when dividends are legally unpayable, namely when the corporation's capital is depleted. In this way, an inquiry into the corporation's solvency, or the adequacy of its capital, at the time of the transaction seems unavoidable, making the fiduciary-duty analysis dovetail with the constructive fraudulent-transfer analysis. For this reason, there may be few cases in which fiduciary-duty law provides relief for asset stripping that would not also be available through fraudulent-transfer law.

1.4 Veil Piercing

An alternative common-law creditor remedy that can be employed to police asset stripping is piercing the corporate veil. This remedy suspends the normal corporate rule of limited shareholder liability by permitting a creditor to recover an unpaid corporate debt from a controlling shareholder. Courts consider it to be an extraordinary remedy, requiring the creditor to show, first, that the shareholder treated the corporation as his "alter

20 *Id., see also* Quadrant Structured Prods. Co. *v.* Vertin, C.A. No. 6990 (Del. Ch. May 4, 2015).

ego," and, second, that denying recovery for the creditor would sanction fraud or promote injustice.[21]

Most veil-piercing claims founder on the first prong – the alter-ego requirement. To satisfy it, the creditor must show that the corporation's managers completely disregarded corporate formalities. The relevant formalities include electing directors and holding board meetings, adopting bylaws, calling shareholder meetings, and maintaining separate corporate accounts. Only if numerous such formalities were consistently neglected will a court hold that the shareholder indeed treated the corporation as his mere "alter ego."

The difficulty of establishing this first prong explains why veil-piercing claims are rarely successful, particularly when brought against shareholders of publicly traded companies. Public companies usually employ lawyers who admonish the managers to perform all legally germane corporate rituals. Also, the need to have auditors approve financial statements that will be published online and filed with the Securities Exchange Commission compels public companies to comply with bookkeeping standards. It is thus unsurprising that the examiner's report in the Caesars case does not mention veil piercing as a possible source of relief. Successful veil-piercing actions are almost always brought against the owners of small, private companies.

The second prong of the veil-piercing test – the promotion of fraud or some other injustice – is broad and imprecisely defined. It seems to serve as a doctrinal means for denying recovery to creditors in situations in which the alter-ego test is satisfied but the corporation nonetheless ended up bankrupt for legitimate business reasons rather than misconduct by the shareholder. To satisfy it, the creditor can show that the shareholder deliberately misled creditors, invested no capital in the firm, or pulled assets out in anticipation of bankruptcy.[22] In other words, it is likely to be easily satisfied in any asset-stripping fact pattern.

1.5 Substantive Consolidation

Substantive consolidation is a remedy used by bankruptcy trustees to simplify proceedings and, sometimes, amend perceived injustices in the distribution of value among claimants. Under it, the trustee disregards the legal boundaries separating affiliated corporate entities, combining their balance sheets for purposes of determining creditor payout entitlements. When the affiliated entities have different asset/debt ratios, the remedy shifts value from creditors of entities with higher ratios to creditors of those with lower ratios. Most instances of substantive consolidation involve affiliated entities that have entered bankruptcy together. On occasion, however, courts will allow a trustee to use the remedy to pull a non-bankrupt affiliate into a bankruptcy proceeding, making its assets available

21 Sea-Land Services, Inc. *v.* Pepper Source, 941 F.2d 519 (7th Cir. 1991).

22 *See, e.g.,* Kinney Shoe *v.* Polan, 939 F.2d 209 (4th Cir. 1991).

to the creditors of the bankrupt debtor. It is in this application that the remedy might be used to remedy asset stripping.

Bankruptcy courts like substantive consolidation because it simplifies things. Corporate groups often fail to keep accurate entity-level financial records, as their shareholders and securities regulators typically care only about consolidated results. As a consequence, there is often considerable uncertainty about which assets and debts properly belong to which entities in a bankrupt corporate group.[23] Untangling the group's inner affairs can be lucrative for lawyers and accountants, but it harms creditors collectively, as the fees for these professionals are administrative expenses that deplete the estate. To avoid such fees, courts often treat the group as one entity for bankruptcy purposes.

Appellate courts, by contrast, are not so fond of substantive consolidation. No provision of the Bankruptcy Code explicitly permits it, and it seems to rearrange arbitrarily the entitlements granted creditors by state law. Appeals courts therefore admonish bankruptcy judges to apply the remedy sparingly.[24] An oft-cited opinion by the United States Court of Appeals for the Third Circuit, based in Philadelphia, Pennsylvania, holds that substantive consolidation is appropriate only when creditors relied on the combined creditworthiness of the group's members, or when consolidation would make all creditors better off.[25] Neither of these conditions is easy to prove, as the first requires a showing that creditors were ignorant of the existence of multiple debtor entities, and the second typically founders upon the fact that consolidation is highly redistributive in nature and therefore almost always makes some creditors worse off.

Substantive consolidation is even rarer when one of the entities is not a debtor in bankruptcy. Although a few bankruptcy courts have permitted this type of consolidation, the trend in recent cases is in the other direction. Indeed, one bankruptcy court in the Seventh Circuit recently held that consolidation of non-debtor (meaning non-bankrupt) entities is *never* permissible.[26] It is therefore unsurprising that the examiner in the Caesars case, filed in a bankruptcy court in the Seventh Circuit, did not mention the possibility of substantive consolidation of CEOC with any of its non-bankrupt affiliates.

1.6 *Strategic Asset Withholding: The Two-Legged Stool Problem*

During the meeting, several of my distinguished fellow presenters described another form of debtor opportunism that has been observed in Continental jurisdictions, including Belgium and the Netherlands. Under this maneuver, a controlling shareholder places most of a business's assets, along with all its debt, into an insolvency proceeding, but

23 *See* R. Squire, Strategic Liability in the Corporate Group, *The University of Chicago Law Review*, Vol. 78, No. 4, 2011, pp. 605, 616 (collecting sources).

24 *Id.*

25 In re Owens Corning, 419 F.3d 195, 208-209 (3d Cir. 2005).

26 In re: Concepts America, Inc., No. 14 B 34232 (Bankr. N.D. Ill. May 3, 2018).

holds back a key asset such as intellectual property (IP) rights. The shareholder's possession of the key asset gives him an advantage in the subsequent auction for the bankrupt company, as other prospective buyers will be unwilling to bid the full value for the business without access to the key asset, which the shareholder strategically withholds. As a consequence, the shareholder can buy the business back at a low price, shorn of its debts. The useful analogy of a three-legged stool was offered, whereby the shareholder unscrews one leg and puts the rest of the stool into bankruptcy. Naturally, the stool has little utility without the third leg, but this is not for sale.

Before the conference, I had not heard of cases under American law involving the two-legged stool maneuver. My impression was that this form of debtor opportunism is not common in the United States. After the conference, I discussed the matter with a top corporate-bankruptcy lawyer in New York, who has decades of experience in cases involving both large and small business debtors. He confirmed my impression that the maneuver is rare in the United States, and he offered several explanations.

Evidently, the most important safeguard against the two-legged stool maneuver in the United States is the widespread use of secured debt. Most business debtors enter bankruptcy in the United States with their assets already fully encumbered. The secured lenders are typically sophisticated institutional investors who perform extensive due diligence before extending credit and demand a representation that all key assets have been disclosed and made subject to their liens. Since an asset remains encumbered even if its nominal owner changes, such lenders continue to have recourse to their borrower's key assets notwithstanding a shareholder's holding them in a legal entity other than the debtor. The shareholder would thus be unable to retain possession of the asset unless the secured lenders were repaid in full.

With respect to IP rights in particular, there is another safeguard against the two-legged stool maneuver, which is the doctrine that a debtor's estate encompasses all property in which the debtor has any legal or practical interest. Therefore, if a debtor paid for the development of a piece of IP, the bankruptcy trustee would likely be able to argue successfully that it is part of the estate even if it was not formally owned by the debtor at the time of the bankruptcy filing.

The risk of two-legged-stool opportunism might be greatest in the United States with respect to the real estate used by small business entities. The reason is that many such entities do not own the land they operate upon, instead leasing it from their controlling shareholder. When the entity enters bankruptcy, the land remains the property of the controller. Smart lenders protect themselves in this situation by insisting that the debtor have leasing rights that will not terminate upon default and that can be sold along with the rest of its assets in case of a bankruptcy sale.

1.7 Summary of Observations

Under American law, the most reliable correctives for asset stripping in corporate groups are fraudulent-transfer law and the law of fiduciary duties. Both appear to have been potent in the bankruptcy of Caesars Entertainment Operating Company, perhaps the most prominent American asset-stripping case in the last five years. The court-appointed examiner believed that the bankrupt entity could use these sources of relief to recover large amounts from its parent company and affiliates for prebankruptcy transactions that seemed intended to siphon value out of the entity before its bankruptcy filing. The reorganization plan ultimately confirmed by the court distributed value in a manner suggesting that the parties agreed with the examiner's assessment. Veil piercing and substantive consolidation can also be used to remedy asset stripping, but they are less likely to be effective, especially in cases involving public companies with sophisticated legal counsel, or where recovery would have to be obtained from an entity that is not a debtor in bankruptcy.

2 SELECTIVE PERFORATION BY MEANS OF GUARANTEES

As noted earlier, selective bankruptcy of affiliated entities is unusual in the United States. When one member of a corporate group enters bankruptcy, its affiliates tend to fall in with it. Widespread use of intragroup guarantees – whereby group members guarantee each other's debts to outside lenders – contributes to these group bankruptcies by tying members' fortunes together.

In these group bankruptcies, an important question is whether the intragroup guarantees are enforceable. If they are, then the lenders who received them will typically recover significantly more than they would otherwise, at the expense of general creditors. The standard American rule is that a lender holding a guarantee can "prove" the full amount of his claim against both the borrower and the guarantor. In other words, if he is owed $100 on the loan, he can submit a $100 claim against each of the borrower and the guarantor, rather than submitting the full $100 claim against only one of these entities, and then a claim for the deficiency, if any, against the other. The number of full claims that can be so asserted may be increased without limit, simply by adding more guarantees from other affiliates, to the point that the lender recovers close to 100% of his claim even when most other creditors recover only pennies on the dollar.[27] For this reason, the enforceability of intragroup guarantees among codebtors can make a drastic difference in the relative size of creditor recoveries.

27 The sum of the lender's recoveries on these various claims is not, however, permitted to exceed the total amount he is owed.

2.1 *Economic Overview of the Problem*

The intragroup guarantee has two main functions. They could be called "defensive" and "offensive," but a more precise pair of terms would be *protective* and *opportunistic.* The first function – the protective – is economically efficient, and the law should protect it. The second use – the opportunistic – is value destroying and should be suppressed. Unfortunately, American courts do not adjudicate challenges to intragroup guarantees in a manner that tracks this distinction.

The protective use of intragroup guarantees is a response to the first topic of our conference – asset stripping. A lender to a member of a corporate group suffers if the group's managers transfer value out of the member, because the transfer increases the lender's expected loss contingent upon default. If, however, the lender has a guarantee from (for example) the subsidiary's parent (this would be a "downstream" guarantee), then he is largely indifferent to the division of value between the parent and the subsidiary. As more group members also guarantee the lender's claim, his scope of indifference widens.

Asset stripping is an example of the type of conduct that generates what Michael Jenson and William Meckling, in an influential 1976 paper, called "the agency costs of debt."[28] These costs arise when debt induces a company to take actions that enrich the company's shareholders not by increasing wealth but by shifting value away from creditors. For example, by transferring assets from Sub A to Sub B, sibling members of a hypothetical corporate group, the group's managers can reduce Sub B's cost of debt, benefiting the group's shareholders. But no economic value has been created: the shareholders' gain came at the expense of Sub A's creditors, whose claims are now riskier. To prevent such transfers, Sub A's creditors might incur monitoring costs. And the group's managers might incur bonding costs to reassure Sub A's creditors that the transfers will not occur. Finally, if the transfer occurs anyway, Sub B may engage in overinvestment due to the artificial reduction in its cost of credit (subsidized involuntarily by Sub A's creditors).[29] These three types of cost – monitoring costs, bonding costs, and overinvestment – collectively constitute the agency costs of debt.

The agency costs of debt destroy wealth by eroding the joint surplus from credit arrangements. Therefore, holding other factors constant, measures that reduce agency costs should be encouraged. Intragroup guarantees, when deployed for protective purposes, are an example of such measures. If Sub B were to guarantee Sub A's outside debts, then the group's managers would be unable to increase Sub B's creditworthiness by shifting value

28 M.C. Jensen & W.H. Meckling, "Theory of the Firm: Managerial Behavior, Agency Costs and Ownership Structure," *Journal of Financial Economics*, Vol. 3, No. 4, 1976, p. 305.

29 Overinvestment is the committing of capital to a project whose expected value to equity holders is positive but net expected impact on all parties is negative. It occurs when the parties who fund the project expect losses, if they occur, to be borne by third parties.

from Sub A to Sub B. Each transfer from A to B would bring with it a commensurate increase in B's liability on its guarantees to A's lenders. Assuming they know about the guarantees, potential creditors of Sub B would take into account the financial conditions of Sub A before lending to Sub B. Since asset stripping would be ineffective, it would be less likely, and the agency costs of debt would fall.

Protecting lenders against opportunistic asset shifting is not, however, the only function of the intragroup guarantee. It also has its opportunistic function, which is to increase the expected recovery of the beneficiary at the expense of other creditors when the corporate group is insolvent, due to the guaranteed lender's ability to submit multiple claims against the estate on the same underlying debt. To prevent this value transfer, the other creditors may incur monitoring costs. To reassure them that this potential dilution of their recoveries will not occur, the debtor may incur bonding costs. Finally, if the expected transfer occurs anyway, overinvestment is a hazard. We thus see that the opportunistic use of the intragroup guarantee increases the agency costs of debt, even while its protective use reduces them.

The intragroup guarantee tends to shift value from the guarantor's general creditors to the guaranteed lender because the insolvency risks of members of corporate groups tend to be highly, positively correlated. To see this, consider again the hypothetical in which lenders to Sub B demand guarantees from Sub A. The guarantees make the loans safer, permitting Sub B to pay lower interest rates on its debts. Since this benefit comes at Sub A's expense, either Sub B or the lenders should make payments to Sub A as compensation. Such payments would be analogous to the premiums on insurance policies, as Sub A is insuring Sub B's debts to outside lenders. In practice, such compensating payments for intragroup guarantees are rarely made. But even if they are, it can be shown mathematically that the value of the payments will be insufficient to offset the increased risk to Sub A's creditors whenever the insolvency risks of the two entities are positively correlated, as they almost always will be.[30]

Correlation matters because it creates a "heads I win, tails you lose" relationship between the group's shareholders and the guarantor's general creditors. As long as the group remains solvent, its shareholders benefit from the lower borrowing costs on the guaranteed debt. But if the group becomes insolvent, the shareholders will be indifferent to the triggering of the guarantee, as their equity interest in the guarantor will then be wiped out anyway. The guarantor's creditors benefit (in theory) from the premium paid for the guarantee, but the expected value to them of this benefit, at the time the guarantee is issued, will be insufficient to offset their expected loss, due to the correlation. The result is a net value transfer from the guarantor's general creditors to the guaranteed lender, which the group's managers can capture for the shareholders by adjusting the interest rate on the loan.

30 Squire, 2011, pp. 624-628.

There is an analogy here to secured lending. When a debtor grants a lien on his property to a lender, he protects that lender against various forms of debtor misconduct. At the same time, however, the lien increases the riskiness of the debtor's other loans. Thus, the arrangement has both protective and opportunistic functions. The secured lender is willing to pay a lower interest rate, which potentially enhances the debtor's asset value. But this enhanced value will not be sufficient to offset the expected losses to the unsecured creditors attributable to the secured creditor's higher recovery if the debtor becomes insolvent. A secured loan is thus like an intragroup guarantee, capable of both reducing and increasing the agency costs of debt. But the increase in the agency costs due to opportunism is even greater for intragroup guarantees than for secured debt. Unlike a secured loan, an intragroup guarantee is enforceable even if no notice of the arrangement was filed in a public registry. Therefore, the monitoring costs for intragroup guarantees are higher.

It should be further noted that a corporate group need not issue any intragroup guarantees in order for there to be an increase in the agency costs of debt attributable to their opportunistic use. The mere option for a group to issue such guarantees may cause lenders to incur monitoring costs and the group to incur bonding costs. For example, lenders may insist on loan covenants prohibiting the issuance of guarantees and then monitor for compliance, while the group may pay for audited financial statements attesting that no such guarantees have been issued. Remedies in bankruptcy that make such monitoring and bonding efforts unnecessary will reduce the agency costs of debt, as long as their application is predictable.

2.2 *Intragroup Guarantees and Fraudulent-Transfer Law*

Intragroup guarantees are frequent targets of constructive fraudulent-transfer claims in bankruptcy proceedings. The success of such challenges depends on the type of guarantee and on fact-intensive questions such as whether the trustee can establish that the guarantor was solvent when the guarantee was issued. If he can, then the case will turn on whether the guarantor received a reasonably equivalent value when it issued the guarantee.

The type of guarantee matters for its enforceability. If it is upstream (subsidiary guarantees the debt of parent) or cross-stream (one subsidiary guarantees the debt of another), then the lender defending the guarantee will have to show some kind of benefit to the guarantor entity, as distinct from the benefits to the borrower and lender, to defeat the fraudulent-transfer challenge. It is well established that a benefit to a third party cannot satisfy the reasonably-equivalent value requirement for purposes of constructive fraudulent-transfer law.

As noted above, the Bankruptcy Code defines "value" for purposes of fraudulent-transfer analysis as property received or the satisfaction or securing of a debt previously incurred. If courts followed this text strictly, they would rarely find that cross-stream and upstream guarantees satisfied it, as corporate managers almost never bother to arrange for a direct payment to the guarantor entity as consideration for an intragroup guarantee. Sometimes, however, courts find that the guarantor received "indirect" value, most commonly because the guarantee made possible a loan that had the potential to keep the group as a whole, including the guarantor, out of bankruptcy. However, a recent, prominent decision by the Eleventh Circuit Court of Appeals, based in Atlanta, Georgia, cast doubt on the legal relevance of such indirect benefits.[31] As a result, bankruptcy courts may increasingly stick to the statutory text and insist on a direct benefit, such as a premium paid to the guarantor.

Downstream guarantees are a different animal. Conceiving parents and subsidiaries as having an "identity of interests," courts have consistently held that downstream guarantees automatically confer a benefit on the guarantor, the parent, because they reduce the borrowing costs of the subsidiary, which redounds to the advantage of the parent through its equity interest in the subsidiary.[32] As a consequence, downstream guarantees have largely been immune in bankruptcy to attack as constructive fraudulent transfers. As the purpose of fraudulent-transfer law is to protect creditors, this manner of analyzing downstream guarantees is unfortunate. As I have shown in my scholarship, downstream guarantees often produce larger wealth transfers away from the guarantor's general creditors, and thus contribute more to the agency costs of debt, than do otherwise similar cross-stream guarantees.[33] The reason is that the parent's equity interest in the subsidiary increases the correlation between the risk that the subsidiary will become insolvent and the risk that the parent will. The enhanced equity value of the parent due to the guarantee is of little consolation to its creditors, as this equity interest is likely to be wiped out when the subsidiary defaults on its debts, triggering the guarantee. A better approach would be for courts to hew to the statutory language limiting "value" to property or the satisfaction of a debt, as a mere reduction in a subsidiary's borrowing costs would not fall under either of these categories.

Unfortunately, the distinctions that courts currently rely on to resolve fraudulent-transfer challenges to intragroup guarantees bear little relation to considerations of economic efficiency. The blanket immunity for downstream guarantees is ambiguous in its effects, as we cannot tell in general whether the protective benefits of such guarantees typically outweigh their opportunism costs. A similar ambiguity applies to cross-stream and upstream guarantees, with the added complication that there is little relationship between the guarantees' net economic impact on general creditors and the manner in

31 In re Tousa, 680 F.3d 1298 (11th Cir. 2012).

32 *See, e.g.,* In re Royal Crown Bottlers of N. Am., Inc., 23. B.R. 28 (Bankr. N.D. Ala. 1982).

33 Squire, 2011, p. 636.

which courts assess the equivalent-value requirement. Notably, even if the guarantor received a premium equaling the full value of the guarantee to the lender – which would presumably satisfy the equivalent-value requirement as most courts interpret it – the guarantor's general creditors would still experience a net decrease in the value of their claims.

2.3 *Relationship to Substantive Consolidation*

Under substantive consolidation, intragroup obligations are typically canceled, and intragroup guarantees are as well. Naturally, the canceling of a guarantee redistributes value away from the lender whose debt was guaranteed, as he can no longer submit multiple proofs of claim on the same underlying debt. From the perspective of economy efficiency, this seems to be an ideal result. Consolidation erases the consequences of asset shifting within the group, thus serving the same protective function as the intragroup guarantee. At the same time, it prevents the type of opportunistic wealth transfer in favor of the guaranteed lender that itself generates the agency costs of debt.

To be sure, substantive consolidation can undermine other economic benefits of the corporate form. In particular, creditors may have relied on the boundaries between group entities to economize on their information costs, as these partitions permit creditors to base the terms of lending on the creditworthiness of particular entities within the group rather than the group overall. Regular application of substantive consolidation would undermine this informational benefit. It should be noted, however, that intragroup guarantees also undermine informational efficiencies. If Sub B has guaranteed the debts of Sub A, then Sub B's creditors will have to take Sub A's creditworthiness into account when lending to Sub B, as they will be forced to share Sub B's assets with Sub A's lender if the corporate group enters bankruptcy. Therefore, the issuance of intragroup guarantees is evidence that a group's creditors did not use the legal boundaries between group members to economize on their information costs, and thus that substantively consolidating the group would not destroy economic value.

Unfortunately, one of the leading appellate decisions on substantive consolidation holds that the presence of intragroup guarantees should make a bankruptcy court less, rather than more, willing to apply the remedy. The logic of the opinion was that consolidation, and hence the canceling of the guarantees, would deny lenders the benefit of the guarantees for which they had bargained.[34] Under this view, the opportunistic function of intragroup guarantees is just as worthy of judicial protection as the protective function.

The holding is vulnerable to criticism on several grounds. For one thing, the division of a bankruptcy estate among creditors is a zero-sum proposition: a higher recovery for one creditor necessarily means lower recoveries for others. In that setting, enforcing an

34 In re Owens Corning, 419 F.3d 195, 208-209 (3d Cir. 2005).

intragroup guarantee, so that the lender gets the "benefit of the bargain," perforce means that other creditors receive less of what they had bargained for. After all, they also bargained for a contractual promise that the debtor would pay them what they were owed. A perhaps wiser approach would be to determine recoveries based on rules that reduce the agency costs of debt *ex ante*. One such rule would be to treat the presence of intragroup guarantees as grounds for substantively consolidating affiliated debtors while prohibiting lenders who have received guarantees from putting in more than one proof of claim against the consolidated estate.

The court in the aforementioned case was under the impression that the lenders would not have extended credit to the corporate group unless they had expected to receive the full protections accorded by the guarantees. The court treated such reluctance as a reason that the guarantees should be enforced. From the perspective of economic efficiency, however, the correct result is the opposite. If a borrower and lender cannot reach mutually advantageous loan terms except through an arrangement that shifts risk onto third parties (the borrower's general creditors), then the loan is economically wasteful, as it is being used to fund overinvestment. The inability of a firm to borrow in some contexts is, to take a phrase from the computer business, a feature rather than a bug. It is evidence that the firm is not creditworthy, as the firm is unable to identify projects whose returns will be sufficient to justify the risks they impose on all parties.

The failure of courts to see the virtues of this market constraint on lending is a symptom of the common view that bankruptcy is a fate so terrible for creditors that firms should be permitted to take almost any measure to avoid it. In fact, bankruptcy is a creditor-protection arrangement. Debtor efforts to avoid it through "gambling for resurrection"—investing in low-probability, high-upside projects—typically reduce the expected value of creditor claims instead of increasing them. Put another way, gambling for resurrection is, like asset stripping, a form of debtor misconduct that generates the agency costs of debt. Courts should therefore not let firms use intragroup guarantees to engage in it.

2.4 Summary of Observations

Given that they have both protective and opportunistic functions, with opposing implications for the agency costs of debt, intragroup guarantees present special problems for lawmakers who care about economic efficiency. Intragroup guarantees are often challenged as constructive fraudulent transfers, but the factual inquiries that such challenges entail are unlikely to reveal whether the guarantees in question were, on net, value creating or value destroying at the time they were issued. Therefore, a better approach is to use the presence of intragroup guarantees as grounds for substantively consolidating the borrower and guarantor entities, assuming both are already in bankruptcy. This remedy protects creditors against asset shifting – the value-creating function of intragroup guarantees – while avoiding the opportunistic wealth transfers that enforcement of intragroup guarantees often deliver.

Curb Your Opportunism: Limits to Group Structures and Asset Partitioning in Insolvency in Belgium

*Joeri Vananroye, Arie Van Hoe and Gillis Lindemans**

1 Introduction

1.1 Terminology

Asset partitioning refers to limited liability (or owner shielding) and entity shielding. In both cases a pool of assets is allocated to a pool of liabilities. The economic justifications of limited liability and entity shielding typically refer – sometimes implicitly – to the situation of a legal with *many* shareholders and with a business that is solely owned by that *one* legal entity.

Hansmann and Squire refer to this type of asset partitioning as *external asset partitioning.*[1] Asset partitioning is also used within a business to make separate pools of assets and liabilities; this is *internal asset partitioning.*[2] A classical example is the corporate group that has a business shattered over many entities, most of which have directly or indirectly the parent company as single (or dominant) shareholder. The distinction between external and internal asset partitioning is not set in stone. In this paper we will consider the situation of a company owned (or primarily owned) by a single shareholder as internal asset partitioning, even if that shareholder is a physical person. The economic unity between the single shareholder and the business of her company is similar to, if not stranger than, that between the separate entities of a corporate group.

Asset partitioning builds walls between pools of assets and liabilities. Sometimes, the insiders themselves disregard the asset partitioning that they have set up themselves. This is referred to as *selective de-partitioning.* A crude example is the single shareholder or the

---

* Prof. Dr. Joeri Vananroye, KU Leuven, TPR leerstoelhouder at Leiden University, attorney at the Brussels Bar.
Arie Van Hoe, University of Antwerp, attorney at the Brussels Bar.
Dr. Gillis Lindemans, KU Leuven, attorney at the Brussels Bar.

1 H. Hansmann & R. Squire, "External and Internal Asset Partitioning: Corporations and Their Subsidiaries, The Oxford Handbook of Corporate Law and Governance (Forthcoming)"; Yale Law & Economics Research Paper No. 535. Available at: https://ssrn.com/abstract=2733862, p. 2.

2 *Id.*

parent company extracting assets from its company or subsidiary or shifting liabilities toward it. A more sophisticated example is a guarantee of one entity of a group toward another entity of the group. Often, legal rules provide the creditors of the shareholders of a company with remedies against selective de-partitioning. In such a case, the law reinforces the walls of asset partitioning.

Sometime the law also tears down or pierces the walls of asset partitioning in order to protect the creditors of a company. This is referred to as *remedial de-partitioning.* An example of an extreme remedial de-partitioning technique is piercing the corporate veil or substantive consolidation of the insolvency of a group.

With an eye on the insolvency of the business of a group, the insiders can set up asset partitioning in such a way as to extract value from the creditors of the separate legal entities. This is referred to as *artificial asset partitioning.* The crudest form of artificial asset partitioning is transferring value to entities that are insolvency remote in the vicinity of an insolvency procedure. A more sophisticated form of artificial asset partitioning consists of keeping an asset that is vital for the going concern value of the business (*e.g.*, intellectual property (IP) rights or real estate) in an entity that is insolvency remote and use this as leverage in the case of a sale of the business in an insolvency procedure. This can be done by bidding at an artificially depressed price (as no other bidders will be interested without the vital asset) or by trying to allocate as much as possible of the global purchase price to the insolvency remote asset.

1.2 Overview

Chapter 1 examines the Belgian approach to asset partitioning, and Chapter 2 highlights techniques (such as directors' liability) that remedy the negative aspects of asset partitioning in general. Chapter 3 illustrates how these techniques can be used for remedial de-partitioning in the case of internal asset partitioning (single shareholders companies or group companies). Chapter 4 looks at remedies against selective de-partitioning, with intragroup guarantees as a case-study. This chapter will also indicate how Belgian tax law is entity focused, thus encouraging internal asset partitioning while at the same time putting strong limits on selective de-partitioning. Chapter 5 looks at the treatment of internal asset partitioning in insolvency law, which has de-partitioning techniques (such as consolidation of the insolvency of separate group entities) and remedies against artificial asset partitioning. We conclude that chapter by observing that the justification for selective de-partitioning (*i.e.*, the existence of a group going concern value transcending the separate entities) could also justify more far-reaching remedial de-partitioning rules in the case of a group insolvency.

2 Asset Partitioning in General

2.1 The Traditional Distrust of Asset Partitioning...

Belgian private law is traditionally very distrustful of asset partitioning in the shape of both limited liability and entity shielding. It has inherited from the 19th century French doctrine (Aubry & Rau) the idea that: (i) only persons have an estate; and (ii) every person has only one estate.[3] An "estate" ("*vermogen*" / "*patrimoine*") is a pool of assets that serves as collateral for a pool of liabilities. Accordingly, the traditional *théorie du patrimoine* entails that a person cannot have separate pools of assets that serve as collateral for separate pools of liabilities. This theory betrays a strong distrust of asset partitioning, both internal and external.

The legal basis for this view is found in Article 7 and Article 8 of the Mortgage Act of 16 December 1851 (inserted as Title XVIII in the Belgian Civil Code). Article 7 states: "Every person who is personally obligated is liable with all his assets, either moveable or immovable, both present and future, to make good on his obligations." Article 8 states: "The assets of the debtor are joint collateral of his creditors, and their price will be distributed amongst them pari passu, unless there is a legitimate cause of priority." The "legitimate cause of priority" is understood to refer to security interests and statutory preferential rights. The principles laid down in these provisions are considered to be mandatory rules relating to public policy (*ordre public).*

Over time, more legal instruments have been recognized as a "legitimate cause of priority." Where it used to be the case that there had to be an unequivocal statutory basis, legal authors and case law now acknowledge that other legal instruments or entities (such as partnerships or joint property) can be a ground for a cause of priority (in the examples given: for the partnership creditors or the joint creditors). Also, the legislature has recognized separate pools of assets within an estate (such as the trust account of certain professionals, *e.g.*, lawyers). Yet the 19th century principle of '*one person, one and only one estate*' remains a solid and important rule of positive law.

The draft provisions Articles 35 and 36 of a new book on property law in the Belgian Civil Code, recently submitted to Parliament, reaffirm current Articles 7 and 8 of the Mortgage Act and can be seen as a codification of the traditional *théorie du patrimoine.*

---

3 W. Van Gerven, *Algemeen deel*, Story, Brussels, 1987, 238, nr. 87. It should be noted that the *théorie du patrimoine* of Aubry & Rau is more nuanced and less carved in stone than generally presented by modern French or Belgian authors. *See, e.g.*, C. Aubry & C. Rau, *Cours de droit civil français d'après la méthode de Zachariae*, VI, Paris, Marchal & Billard, 1873, §574, pp. 232-234.

2.2 *... Hides a Liberal Approach to Asset Partitioning, Provided a Corporate Form Is Used*

The image that appears when looking at private law in isolation is one of strong distrust of asset partitioning. Yet this image changes substantially when company law is taken into account.

In the beginning of the 19th century, the rule "one person, one and only one estate" was generally understood as referring to *natural persons*. The incorporation of legal persons, particularly of legal persons with owner shielding (limited liability), was exceptional and restricted. It was limited to certain types of activities and subject to governmental authorization.[4]

Over time, the restrictions on the incorporation of legal persons have been considerably relaxed. Milestones in this evolution have been the abolishment of the required governmental authorization for public companies (1873), the introduction of a nonprofit form with legal personality and limited liability (1921), the opening of the for-profit forms for all kinds of activities (1926), the introduction of a private form with legal personality and limited liability (1935), and the authorization of single-shareholder companies (1987). The new Code for Companies and Associations, which entered into force on 1 May 2019 and submitted to royal assent, eliminates minimal capital requirements, and mandatory pay-up rules for the BV/SRL, which is set to become the most commonly used corporate form, will be eliminated.

As a result, the 19th century doctrine of "one person, one and only one estate," while at face value barely modified, presently has completely different practical consequences. Presently, a natural person can easily incorporate, control, and benefit from one *or more* legal persons. The traditional motto should now be understood as "one natural person can possibly have many other estates through the fiction of other legal persons." Put differently: direct asset partitioning is frowned upon; indirect asset partitioning (through the use of legal persons) is easily available.

This raises the important question: Why is the traditional animus against asset partitioning not an issue, or less so, in cases where the technique of the corporate form with legal personality is used to bring about such asset partitioning?

---

4 *See*, E.W. Orts, *Business Persons. A Legal Theory of the Firms*, Oxford, Oxford University Press, 2013: "*On this ancient view, business firms exist only at the behest and at the pleasure of government.*"

3 The Legal Technology Mitigating the Negative Effects of Asset Partitioning

3.1 *The Redeeming Virtues of the Corporate Form with Legal Personality*

The technique of the corporate form with legal personality comes with the following features that remedy the negative effects of asset partitioning: (i) publicity, (ii) seizure of shares, (iii) priority of company creditors (including techniques of attributing liabilities to the company), (iv) directors' liability (including corporate benefit tests), (v) accounting rules, and (vi) insolvency procedures.

These features explain two things. Firstly, they explain why the technique of the corporate form with legal personality suffers less from the traditional animus against asset partitioning than other techniques (*e.g.*, in property or contract law) that do not come with (all of) these features. Secondly, they explain why the corporate form has become more liberalized in the 19th and 20th centuries. Each of the techniques has been fine-tuned significantly in the course of that period.

These features also set an agenda for corporate reform: the efficiency of each of them can still be improved further.

In a next chapter of this report, we will see how each of these techniques plays or could play a role in remedial de-partitioning (with a focus on internal partitioning).

3.2 *Publicity*

Arguably the most important change in corporate law since the 19th century is the advancement of the technology that gives publicity to shareholders' arrangements. It has become considerably easier to set up, feed, and consult a company register. At the beginning of the 19th century, a creditor from Brussels who wanted to check the arrangements of a company in Bruges was in for a long journey on horseback through remote and unsavory regions. Even until late in the 20th century, such a check involved browsing (without the help of an easy search function) many volumes or micro films of an official gazette. Today, a third party interested in the particulars of a specific legal entity can do a quick check online.

A more efficient publicity system is probably the lowest-hanging fruit for corporate reform. The nuts and bolts of a publicity system rarely excite a law professor. That does not make them less relevant. A legal entity has important effects that are binding on third parties, such as entity shielding and limited liability (organizational law is indeed much more important as property law than as contract law[5]). At the very least, those parties should be put on notice through a system that is easy to consult.

Raymond Saleilles, whose *Etude sur l'histoire des sociétés en commandite* is still one of the great contributions to continental company law scholarship (with a focus on asset partitioning), pointed out how asset partitioning became a solid feature of the "partnership en commandite" only with the emergence of a publicity system in company law.[6] Changes in the technology used for disseminating information have arguably been the most important driver of change in company law. Implementing the latest technological developments should therefore always be high on the agenda of any attempt at corporate reform.

However important publicity is to warn third parties about asset partitioning and other proprietary effects of the corporate form, the limits of this remedy should always be considered. Firstly, publicity has only a very limited role in the protection of nonadjusting creditors, *i.e.*, involuntary creditors or creditors with limited bargaining power. Secondly, even the most up-to-date and user-friendly publicity system would still entail considerable transaction costs for third parties who would want to ascertain their situation. Information that is readily retrievable still needs to be consulted and interpreted. Even careful interpretation could still leave some doubt or induce errors. That is why another important trend, which at first sight seems at odds with the increased user-friendliness of the corporate information system, is that third parties are not bound by many provisions in the articles of association, even if they are disclosed in the company register (*e.g.*, First Company Law Directive).

3.3 Seizure of shares

When a debtor owns shares in a company, such shares form part of the debtor's assets and are available for creditors to seek recourse for their unpaid claims.

The legal seizure of shares is both an underestimated cornerstone and an underestimated weak point of asset partitioning using the corporate form. In the corporate form, personal creditors of the contributing shareholder have recourse to a bundle of rights that offsets that personal creditors have to undergo entity shielding and capital lock-in (or liquidation protection) as features of the corporate form binding upon third parties. Other techniques of asset partitioning do not always offer such a bundle of cash rights and decision-making rights that can be seized and sold.

In the French-Belgian legal tradition, the technique of the legal person was restricted during the 19th century to entities with a "for-profit" nature, *i.e.*, entities geared toward

5 H. Hansmann & R. Kraakman, "The Essential Role of Organizational Law," *Yale Law Journal*, 2000, p. 390.

6 R. Saleilles, "Etude sur l'histoire des sociétés en commandite," *Annales de droit commercial*, 1895, pp. 52-53, nr. 24-25.

the distribution of the profits toward members. The distrust of nonprofit entities should be partially understood as a legacy of the French Revolution and the cultural, political, and social struggles of the 19th century (a distrust of intermediary bodies, a hostile attitude toward religious organizations, guilds, and trade unions).[7]

A present-day justification of a positive bias toward "for-profit" entities would be this: the legal obligation to distribute any profits causes the shares of the shareholders to be a valuable bundle of rights; this makes the shares an economically valuable asset that can be seized by the personal creditors of the shareholders, which in turn mitigates the harmful effects of asset partitioning for these personal creditors.

The contemporaneous Belgian approach to nonprofits allows them to organize themselves with asset partitioning. The membership rights are not transferable and cannot be seized. We see the justification for this as follows: the legal system recognizes that there are nonprofit goals that justify asset partitioning, even if this results in the absence of a transferable bundle of rights that could be seized. The rules on nonprofits impose the not-for-profit nature of the entity through the prohibition of any direct distributions or indirect value transfers toward the members or the decision makers. The justification is this: asset partitioning that does not result in assets that serve as collateral for members' creditors is permitted provided the members do not benefit indirectly from the assets of the entity. Members can opt for entity shielding without shares as long as they do not replicate the cash rights of shareholders.

In the corporate form, entity shielding, capital lock-in, and tradability of shares are intimately connected.[8] The theoretical justification is the following: (i) entity shielding and capital lock-in protect the going concern value of the business of the company; (ii) as a result, the value of the business of the company and the value of the shares in the company increase; (iii) personal creditors are harmed because they have no way to go after the assets of the company as a result of entity shielding and capital lock-in, but (iv) in return, they get the possibility to seize the shares, the value of which largely depends on entity shielding and capital lock-in.

The practice, however, is somewhat messier, and a creditor encounters many hurdles on the way to actual seizure of shares:

- ***Form of shares (registered, bearer,...).*** The form of shares is a first important hurdle for creditors aiming to seize them. Bearer shares are in theory relatively easy to seize, as they are moveable assets. In practice, however, bearer shares are almost impossible

7 J. Vananroye, *Morele wezens en wetsontduikende monniken* (opening address at the Belgian Supreme Court on the occasion of the opening of the judicial year 2012), Antwerp, Intersentia, 2012, p. 2, nr. 2.

8 H. Hansmann, R. Kraakman & R. Squire, "Law and the Rise of the Firm," *Harvard Law Review*, 2005-2006, pp. 1353-1354.

to seize as the debtor can hide them, if need be literally, under the carpet.[9] This is one of the reasons why bearer shares have been outlawed in many jurisdictions, including Belgium.[10]

- ***Publicity of share ownership***. Registered shares are more difficult to hide from creditors. Whether creditors will be able to seize registered shares will in practice depend largely on the type of publicity mandated by the applicable company law.[11] Belgium, to take one example, does a very poor job of informing creditors about the shares held by their debtors. Other jurisdictions, such as the Netherlands, organize the publicity of shareholdings in a more easily accessible way.[12] In general, the rules on publicity given to the proprietary aspects of the company (*e.g.*, via registration) and the usability of the publicity system—wrongly perceived as mundane matters by many legal scholars—should be a priority in company law reform.[13]
- ***In rem transfer restrictions***. Restrictions on the transfer of shares (either in company law or in the articles of association or even sometimes in shareholders' agreements) are binding on third parties in many jurisdictions ("*erga omnes* effect of transfer restrictions").[14] Such binding effect can understandably impede the forced sale on behalf of a personal creditor of a shareholder. Some jurisdictions, like the Netherlands, allow transfer restrictions to be set aside if they impede a forced sale under certain conditions.[15] Others, like Belgium, do not have a similar easy way out of transfer restrictions.[16] Moreover, even if a creditor manages to set aside such restrictions, they will still typically negatively affect the share price, given that the potential buyer remains bound by them in the case of resale.

---

9 This has led to the paradoxical observation that the easier it is to seize shares, the harder it is to trace them. K. Geens & M. Wyckaert, *Verenigingen en Vennootschappen. De vennootschap. Algemeen deel*, Mechelen, Kluwer, 2011, 333, para. 175. *See also* K. Geens, "Over veinzing, stromannen en tussenpersonen," *TFR*, 2003, p. 407, text to footnote 32.

10 For Belgium, *e.g.*, *see* the Law of 14 December 2005 on the abolition of bearer shares.

11 J. Armour & M.J. Whincop, "The Proprietary Foundations of Corporate Law," *Oxford Journal of Legal Studies*, 2007, pp. 447, 456.

12 For a comparison between Belgium and the Netherlands, *see* D. Bruloot & K. Maresceau, "Het aandeelhoudersregister in het Belgische recht: toepassingsproblemen en voorstellen tot hervorming," *T.Not*, 2014, pp. 688-729.

13 J. Armour & M.J. Whincop, "The Proprietary Foundations of Corporate Law," *Oxford Journal of Legal Studies*, 2007, p. 464.

14 K. Geens & M. Wyckaert, "Doorwerking van het gemeen contractenrecht in het vennootschappelijk rechtspersonenrecht," *in Vereniging voor de Vergelijkende Studie van het Recht van België en Nederland, Preadviezen 2013*, Boom Juridische Uitgevers, Den Haag, 2013, p. 298.

15 *See* in relation to the *Besloten Vennootschap* (closely held company): Art. 2:195, para. 7 of the Dutch Civil Code. This possibility does not exist for the *Naamloze Vennootschap* (public company), K.K. Buijn & P.M. Storm, *Ondernemingsrecht BV en NV in de praktijk*, Deventer, Kluwer, 2013, p. 212.

16 Legal scholarship has proposed to apply, by analogy, the internal conflict resolution procedures of forced share sale or purchase. This solution, however, is uncertain and in any case requires judicial intervention, *see* R. Tas, "Beslag op aandelen," *in* H. Braeckmans, *De NV in de praktijk*, Antwerp, Kluwer, 2003, pp. 151-152.

- ***Shares in private company are rarely an interesting asset.*** The previous hurdles are legal impediments. Even when there would be no such legal impediments, shares in private companies will rarely be an interesting asset to buy for third parties, in particular if they represent a minority stake.

Because of these legal and *de facto* limits to the transferability of shares, personal creditors can suffer the disadvantages of entity shielding and capital lock-in, without reaping the purported benefits thereof.[17] As a result, company law in many jurisdictions allows personal creditors to trump capital lock-in if the shares are not tradable or tradable subject to important restrictions. This insight was reflected in Article 1865, 4° of the French Civil Code of 1804 (later copied as Article 39, 4° of the Belgian Companies Code and currently surviving barely amended as Article 4:16, third indent of the new Code for Companies and Associations), which automatically mandated the liquidation of the assets of the entity in case a shareholder becomes insolvent. This provision was written for the partnership form, the shares of which are not tradable, but has also been applied by analogy to other company forms with far-reaching restrictions on the transferability of shares.

Hansmann, Kraakman and Squire have identified the costs that entity shielding imposes on the shareholders' personal creditors as the next chapter in the evolution of legal entities.[18] We submit that the difficulties surrounding the seizure of shares are an important and underestimated part of this next chapter in many jurisdictions, including Belgium. Personal creditors often face prohibitive information and search costs. In the absence of a proper publicity system, creditors can easily be left in the dark about the nature and the amount of shareholding of their debtor. Given these legal and factual hurdles, it seems reasonable to say that most personal creditors of shareholders are in fact nonadjusting creditors. While entity shielding is freely imposed on them, the theoretical instruments to mitigate such entity shielding are difficult to implement in practice. This is different for "powerful" creditors, such as financial institutions, who have leverage to (contractually) overcome the negative aspects (for them) of asset partitioning (see below).

17 In many jurisdictions a similar dire situation exists for the personal creditors of spouses. These creditors have to undergo the entity shielding of the joint marital property. As creditors cannot file a claim for divorce or for the partitioning of the marital property, they are also confronted with capital lock-in. At the same time, the share in a "marital association" is, because of its personal nature, not tradable and, hence, cannot be seized and sold by the personal creditors of a spouse. Belgian marital property law tackles this problem by promoting many creditors, who under the general rules of private law would be personal creditors of a spouse, to the status of creditor of the joint estate. Such creditors can go after the joint assets without being hampered by entity shielding. *See* J. Vananroye, "Fifty ways to leave your lover: over verdeling, ontbinding, overdracht en uittreding," *Notarieel en Fiscaal Maandblad*, 2015/5, p. 156, nr. 7.

18 H. Hansmann, R. Kraakman & R. Squire, "Law and the Rise of the Firm," *Harvard Law Review*, 2005-2006, Vol. 119, No. 1335, pp. 1399-1403.

3.4 *Priority of company creditors and rules for the attribution of liabilities toward the corporate entity*

As mentioned earlier, corporate asset partitioning creates a bundle of rights in the estate of the shareholders that serves as collateral for their personal creditors. At the same time, the corporate form results in a separate estate with its own creditors, who have priority over the personal creditors (technically more correct: corporate creditors are the *only* creditors who can seize the corporate assets, and mandatory rules, such as distribution constraints, limit transfers to shareholders unless the rights of corporate creditors are satisfied or reasonably safeguarded).

For a modern reader, the presence of corporate creditors and their priority over personal creditors is such a self-evident feature that it might seem silly to mention it as a defining characteristic of the corporate form. Yet taking a historical perspective, it becomes clear that it was a feature that took time to develop.

The center of the Napoleonic legislature's attention was the *internal* relations among the shareholders themselves, not the external relations between the entity and third parties (including the creditors). This contractual myopia is before anything else revealed by the name given to the relevant title in the *Code civil* ("on the *contract* of company") and its position between other contracts such as the lease and the loan. During the 19th century, the classical French treatises on civil law continued to discuss the partnership and the corporation as part of the "minor contracts" (*les petits contrats*).

In the same vein, the provisions in the *Code civil* on the company display a startling disregard for the position of the creditors and the effects of asset partitioning. In Belgium, these provisions still survive, hardly modified, in the Belgian Company Code as the provisions applicable to partnerships. The new Code for Companies and Associations also recycles many of the provisions of the *Code civil* of 1804.

This disregard is most vividly demonstrated by the lack of any provision (*i*) on the claims of the entity creditors on the entity assets; (*ii*) on the claims of personal creditors on the entity assets prior to dissolution; (*iii*) on the liquidation of the entity (other than one laconic reference in art. 1872 C.c. to the rules on partitioning of the jointly owned inheritances).[19]

In other words, the *Code civil* simply ignored the issue of entity shielding and the priority of corporate creditors altogether. It is revealing that the texts of neither the *Code civil* (1804) nor the *Code de commerce* (1807) use a concept like "legal entity" or "legal personality" (though similar concepts can be found in the preparatory works).[20]

---

19 The rules on partitioning of jointly owned inheritances for their part also focused on the internal relations among the heirs, while being indifferent to the rights of the creditors (and the inheritance creditors in particular).

20 F.M. Huussen-De Groot, *Rechtspersonen in de negentiende eeuw*, Leiden, Universitaire Pers Leiden, 1976, p. 11.

3.5 *Criteria for Attribution of Liability*

While today the presence and priority of entity creditors is no longer an issue – at least in corporate forms with legal personality – Belgian law has still not fully settled which creditors actually qualify as corporate creditors. The rules that attribute claims to corporate entities, directors, shareholders, or other insiders are an important (and again often underestimated) part of organizational law.

For voluntary creditors (such as contractual creditors), the rules are fairly clear, as the rules of agency are used. A contractual liability is attributed to the company if an agent acted (i) in the name of the company and (ii) with authority to bind the company. The main development of the last decades is that third parties can to a large extent disregard (see above) any internal limits to the authority of corporate agents if such limits are not part of normal practice with regard to representation (see, in particular, the First Company Law Directive and the jurisprudence on apparent authority).

The attribution of claims by involuntary creditors (such as tort victims) to a corporate entity was one of the hotly debated issues in 19th century law. While it is fully settled that a corporate entity can be liable for torts (including for damages and penalties resulting from crimes), legal authors still debate which criteria should be used to attribute torts to companies. This seems to be a topic that is more of an issue in legal doctrine and less of an issue in case law.

An important step was taken in 1999 on the occasion of the introduction of criminal liability for corporate entities (including nonprofit entities and partnerships without legal personality). At that time, a statutory criterion for the attribution of crimes was inserted in Article 5 al. 1 of the Belgian Criminal Code:

> A legal person is criminally liable for crimes which are intrinsically linked with the pursuing of the objectives of the legal person or the safeguarding of its interests or which are, based on the particular circumstances, perpetrated on account of the legal person.

We argue that this criterion for the attribution of crimes should be used, and in practice is being used by courts, for the attribution of other kinds of torts.[21]

A striking difference between the attribution of liabilities toward voluntary and involuntary creditors is the use of a *formal* criterion ("in the name of the legal entity") versus a *substantive* criterion ("on account of the legal entity"). Such a difference is justified. Voluntary creditors can in principle choose whether or not they accept the company as their creditor. If they do not like the outcome of a formal attribution criterion, they can refuse

21 This results in an attribution criterion for torts not unlike the one in the Dutch "Kleuterschool Babbel"-case: HR April 6, 1979, *NJ* 1980/34.

to contract, change the conditions of the contract, or bargain for additional contract partners (*e.g.*, through guarantees by shareholders or directors). A distinction must be made in this respect between voluntary/voluntary creditors (with effective bargaining power) and involuntary/voluntary creditors, being creditors who conclude contracts with the company but have no real bargaining power in doing so. While both types of creditors are voluntary creditors, the latter category is so only from a theoretical point of view. Involuntary/voluntary creditors are therefore entitled to special protection.

Another striking difference is that the attribution of a tort liability to a legal entity does not exclude the attribution of liability for the same activity to another legal entity or to physical persons within the organization involved with the activity. Contract liability, on the other hand, lies *only* with the entities or persons identified as contract party in the agreement. It does not, at least not automatically, extend to legal entities that benefit from the contract or to physical persons involved as agents in negotiating, consenting to, or performing the agreement.

3.6 Directors' liability

3.6.1 Directors' Liability as a Brake on Shareholder's Opportunism

Directors' liability is arguably the most important tool of company law to address the risk of opportunistic behavior for third parties linked to asset partitioning.

Belgian law makes a distinction between internal liability of directors toward the company itself and external liability of directors toward third parties for torts committed in the exercise of their function.

It speaks for itself that external liability (which includes liability for wrongful trading) serves the interests of third parties. As a rule, any person to whom a tort can be attributed is liable for that tort. The circumstance that a tort is committed on behalf of a legal entity does, in principle, not exclude or extenuate the liability of the relevant director.

Less understood is that internal directors' liability (toward the company itself) protects not only the shareholders of the company, but also its creditors.[22] A successful liability claim on behalf of the company (as the case may be through a derivate claim or initiated by a liquidator or bankruptcy trustee) will increase the net asset position of the company and hence improve the position of the company creditors. The same is true for shareholders' liability toward the company, though this type of liability is much more exceptional.

Directors' liability is usually understood as a remedy to tackle the agency conflict between shareholders and directors. Yet it plays an important role in the protection of third parties. A striking symptom of the fact that directors' and shareholders' liability

22 J. Vananroye, *Organisatierecht: werfbezoek aan een onvoltooide piramide*, Acta Falconis VII, Antwerp, Intersentia, 2015, pp. 60-61, para. 29.

toward the company does not only protect the shareholders is that the *sole* shareholder and director of a company can also be held liable toward that company. While they are at first sight merely "contractual" remedies for the conflict between shareholders and directors, internal liability rules thus also operate as "proprietary" rules protecting the interests of third parties.[23]

Directors' liability is an important brake on misconduct by shareholders. Shareholders have only a limited area over which they themselves have formal decision-making powers. For most corporate actions, they can only indirectly influence the decision-making of the board though their powers to remove board members or determine their remuneration. Directors' liability, and above all the role the interests of third parties play in determining whether liability is at stake, ensure that directors do not always fully comply with the wishes of the shareholders. For this reason, it makes sense to have mandatory rules that prohibit the general meeting of shareholders from instructing the board or overruling its decisions.[24] At the very least, an approval or instructions by the general shareholders' meeting should not serve as a safe harbor against liability of directors for matters over which they have authority.

Directors of Belgian companies are often themselves legal persons. Belgian tax law, in fact, promotes the use of single-shareholder companies (*see later*). Article 2:55 of the new Code for Companies and Associations (former Article 61 § 1 of the Belgian Company Code) provides that a legal person who is a director needs to appoint a physical person as a representative agent for the directorship and that such representative agent has the same liability toward the company and toward third parties as the director itself. This rule ensures that asset partitioning cannot be used to curtail the efficiency of directors' liability against that very asset partitioning.

We now turn to "corporate benefit" tests that are an important, but not the only, trigger for directors' liability.

3.6.2 Corporate Benefit Tests as a Fiduciary Standard

In Belgium, a company is allowed to enter into a transaction only insofar as such transaction is compatible with the company's best interests. This "best interests" test is a fiduciary standard limiting the powers of the company's directors and officers – and to some extent shareholders – over the company's estate.

Indeed, transactions violating the "corporate interest" may be declared null and void.[25] Creditors can initiate such a nullity action on the grounds of the corporate interest principle on their own behalf, to the extent they are considered as an "interested party"

23 *See also* J. Armour & M.J. Whincop, "The Proprietary Foundations of Corporate Law," *Oxford Journal of Legal Studies*, 2007, p. 453, footnote 104.

24 *See* in Dutch law the Forum Bank-case (HR January 21, 1955, 1959/43).

25 *See* Art. 2:41, 2 of the new Code for Companies and Associations (Art. 64, 3° of the former Companies Code).

for purposes of the Companies Code.[26] If not, they may still enforce the corporate interest principle in an oblique manner, by bringing a derivative claim on behalf of the debtor company.[27] Moreover, directors and other officers engaging in such transactions on behalf of the company may be held liable toward the company and/or the creditors personally. In case the debtor company goes bankrupt, only the bankruptcy trustee is allowed to bring nullity and liability actions on the grounds of the corporate interest principle.

Exactly what is to be understood by the "corporate interest" is the subject of a longstanding and continuing debate.[28] In any case, the corporate interest should arguably *not* be limited to the collective interest of the shareholders. As the company's assets serve primarily as collateral for its creditors, the company's directors and officers should, at least to some extent, also take into account the company's creditors' best interests. A revealing symptom that this approach is also part of Belgian positive law is that the sole shareholder and director of a company also can violate the "corporate interest" by benefiting himself.[29]

3.6.3 Avoidance of Harmful Transactions

In addition, a specific remedy exists for the protection of creditors. As most jurisdictions, Belgium allows a creditor under certain conditions to avoid a transaction of his debtor on the grounds that it prevents full recovery of his claim. This remedy is known as the *actio pauliana*.[30] It is a remedy (i) of a creditor (ii) against the beneficiary (iii) of an act committed by his debtor (iv) with the intent or knowledge of (v) preventing full recovery of the creditor's claim, provided that (vi) either the transaction was gratuitous or the beneficiary acted in bad faith. The *actio pauliana* exists under both general civil law and bankruptcy law. In the latter case, it is exercised by the bankruptcy trustee.[31]

3.6.4 The Subjective Element: "Knowledge" or "Intent"

As can be derived from condition (iv) above, a transaction can be avoided only if the debtor entered into it with the intent to cause harm or with knowledge of its harmful effect, the so-called "subjective element."

Indeed, according to consistent case law of the Belgian Court of Cassation, a creditor initiating an *actio pauliana* must show not only that the challenged transaction has negatively affected his right of recourse, but also that: (a) the debtor entered into the transac-

26 *See* Art. 2:43, first paragraph of the new Belgian Companies Code (Art. 178 of the former Companies Code).

27 On the basis of Art. 1166 of the Belgian Civil Code.

28 For an extensive discussion *see* A. François, *Het vennootschapsbelang in het Belgische vennootschapsrecht: inhoud en grondslagen*, Antwerp, Intersentia, 1999, xxii+795 p.; K. Geens, "De jurisprudentiële bescherming van de minderheidsaandeelhouder tegen door de meerderheid opgezette beschermingsconstructies," *TRV* 1988, extra afl., pp. 1-72.

29 J. Vananroye, "Ook de enige vennoot heeft altijd gezelschap," *TRV*, 2014, p. 425, para. 1.

30 Art. 1167 Belgian Civil Code.

31 Art. XX.114 Belgian Code of Economic Law.

tion with the fraudulent intent to harm his creditors, or (b) the transaction was "abnormal" and the debtor knew or should reasonably have foreseen the harm to his creditors resulting from the transaction.[32]

3.6.5 Substantive Link between Corporate Interest and *Actio Pauliana*

Unlike the "knowledge" requirement, fraudulent "intent" to harm creditors does not necessarily imply that the harm resulting from the challenged transaction was foreseeable at the time of its conclusion. Indeed, such "intent" is typically deduced from the fact that the relevant transaction cannot be justified in the best interests of the debtor. Hence, in the case that the debtor is a company, there is a substantive link between the concept of the "corporate interest" and the "intent" requirement under the *actio pauliana.*[33]

3.6.6 Liability of Shareholders as De Facto Directors

While "piercing the corporate veil" as a separate ground for liability is often discussed in the Belgian literature, it is of limited importance in practice. The lone cases of "piercing" date before the time directors' liability as a tool of creditor protects was set in place as an established set of rules.

Currently, the Belgian law on the duties of a shareholder toward third parties (such as company creditors) as applied by courts could in our view be stated as follows:

- There are no implied shareholders' duties toward third parties beyond the explicit duties imposed by the legislature. Such implied duties would undercut the benefits of limited liability. The interests of third parties are covered by directors' liability.
- The previous point implies that the quality of shareholder does not trigger a higher duty under the general duty of care (the "good house-father" or "bonus pater familias" of tort law). This is surprising: the normal rule of tort law is that a specific role entails specific duties under the general duty of care.
- The previous points also apply to a controlling shareholder and in the context of corporate groups.
- That does not imply that a shareholder can never be liable under the general duty of care. Obviously, he can like any other person violate the general duty of care.
- If, however, a controlling shareholder is held to have been in violation of a duty, he will be punished more harshly than a wrongdoer at arm's length. Damages imposed on a shareholder have a punitive side. This is justified: a controlling shareholder can make sure that the "victim" of his wrongdoing does not use the normal legal actions to go after him. In addition, a controlling shareholder has an exceptional opportunity to cover up his wrongdoings and their consequences.

32 *See*, i.e. Cass. February 19, 2015, *Arr.Cass.* 2015, 473; Cass. 26 October 1989, *Arr.Cass.* 1989-1990, 282; Cass. March 15, 1985, *Arr.Cass.* 1984-1985, 969.

33 G. Lindemans, *Actio pauliana: een remedie met toekomst voor schuldeisers van rechtspersonen*, diss. KU Leuven, 2018, 167, para. 224.

3.7 Accounting (pm)

Abuse of asset partitioning often involves opportunistic shifting with assets and liabilities. Accounting rules curtail such abuse and provide transparency toward third parties; as such, the development of organizations with limited liability and entity shielding depended largely on the development of accounting rules.[34] Generally accepted accounting principles have become a staple of company law only in the course of the 20th century.

3.8 Bankruptcy procedure as enforcement mechanism

The possibility of bankruptcy with the appointment of bankruptcy trustee independent from the shareholders is very important for the enforcement of other remedies against abuse of asset partitioning, in particular directors' liability, the corporate interest, and *actio pauliana*.

Directors' liability ensures that asset partitioning through the corporate form always holds the threat that one of the assets will be a liability claim. The possibility of bankruptcy ensures, in particular, that if the company is administered by a neutral liquidator or bankruptcy trustee, it becomes possible that it turns itself against its controlling shareholder like a corporate version of Frankenstein's monster.

4 Remedial De-partitioning Techniques, In Particular in Case of Internal Asset Partitioning

4.1 Introduction

In this chapter, we will discuss how these techniques surrounding the corporate form can be used as de-partitioning techniques, *i.e.*, to overcome abuse or other negative externalities linked to asset partitioning. We will focus on internal asset partitioning as defined earlier, in particular group companies and single-shareholder companies owned by a natural person.

We will not discuss the role of publicity and accounting rules with respect to internal asset partitioning. This is not to be understood as indicating that these techniques play no role in regulating internal asset partitioning. On the contrary: the focus of Belgian tax law on the separate entities of a group (see below) ensures that every single entity of a group will definitely have separate accounts. The absence of such accounts would be not just a violation of accounting legislation but also a tax violation triggering severe adverse con-

34 H. Hansmann, R. Kraakman & R. Squire, "Law and the Rise of the Firm," *Harvard Law Review*, 2005-2006, p. 1352.

sequence. Accounting may therefore likely play a more prominent role in the Belgian regulation of internal asset partitioning than in systems where the tax rule focuses on the group as economic reality rather than on the entities of the group. In the latter systems, the separate accounts of the entities might be neglected as only the consolidated accounts matter for tax reasons.

4.2 Specific Rules for Single-shareholder Companies, in Particular in the Case of Enforcement of Shares

4.2.1 Rules on Single-Shareholder Companies as a Rule against Internal Asset Partitioning

Belgian law used to have a blanket prohibition on single-shareholder companies. Such a rule can be seen as a rule against asset partitioning with a merely internal function. It reflects the idea that, while asset partitioning can be a good thing, there can also be such a thing as "too much" asset partitioning.

Under the Belgian Company Code, still in force at the time of writing, there are some special rules that apply to single-shareholder companies. A physical person can incorporate only *one* single-shareholder company. For any subsequent single-shareholder company that shareholder incorporates or acquires (other than through inheritance), he becomes liable for all debts of that company. In the NV/SA form, designed for public companies, a single shareholder becomes liable for all debts after a period of one year with one shareholder.

These rules follow the economic logic that the benefits of limited liability are more evident in the case that there are many shareholders: one shareholder is definitely not "many."

The problem with these rules is that they are very easy to circumvent by having a second shareholder with a symbolic stake. The most devious way is to incorporate a single-shareholder company and then to incorporate together with that company a second company. That company, while economically a single-shareholder company, would not be treated as one by the law. In a corporate group, typically the parent holds all the shares but one, and the other share is held by another affiliate.

Because this rule is so easily circumvented, it is often perceived by legal and business practice as a mere formality. It would be possible, however, to design a more realistic rule by defining "single shareholding" in a way that is less easily circumvented (*e.g.*, by using a certain percentage of direct or indirect shareholding as a threshold). This, however, is not the route taken by the new Code for Companies and Associations, which for the common types of legal entities abolishes most of the restrictions on single-shareholder companies.

4.2.2 Nonenforcement of Legal Transfer Limits Shares Held by One Shareholder in Case of Seizure

In the same vein, we think that in a single-shareholder company transfer restrictions on shares should automatically be considered unenforceable in the case of an execution sale triggered by a personal creditor. A transfer restriction serves no goal in a single-shareholder company other than frustrating the execution sale by personal creditors.

Hence, a blanket rule against such restrictions in a single-shareholder company is justified.[35]

In a company with more than one shareholder, transfer restrictions can have legitimate goals, such as protection against a sale to unwanted bedfellows. Accordingly, a more nuanced approach should govern, such as the binding effect of transfer restrictions as a principle, with the possibility for personal creditors to trump such restrictions and/or go after the value of the company's assets by provoking a liquidation.

Belgian law does not yet have such a rule. Nor does it, unlike Dutch law (Article 474g of the Dutch Code on Civil procedure), have a rule that allows a judge to set aside transfer restrictions if they unreasonably frustrate the execution of the shares. As a result, single shareholders can use transfer restrictions in the articles of association as an impediment for a creditor who wants to seize its shares.

4.3 Enterprise Liability toward Involuntary Creditors in a Corporate Group: Crimes, Torts, and Competition Infringements

4.3.1 Torts Are Attributed by Looking at the Substance and Not at the Form

Belgian law uses a substantive – and not a formalcriterion – to attribute crimes and, we argue, torts:

> A legal person is criminally liable for crimes which are intrinsically linked with the pursuing of the objectives of the legal person or the safeguarding of its interests or which are, based on the particular circumstances, perpetrated on account of the legal person (see earlier).

The substantive nature of the criterion to attribute torts implies a strong de-partitioning feature. The attribution of torts follows economic reality, not legal niceties. The criterion for attribution holds the possibility of a type of enterprise liability in practice. "Enterprise

35 J. Vananroye & B. Van Baelen, "Beslag op aandelen: een stroef verhaal," Tijdschrift voor Rechtspersoon en Vennootschap, 2017, p. 392.

liability," using the words of Hansmann and Squire, "allows the creditor of one member of a corporate group to pierce horizontally to reach the assets of other members."[36]

A substantive criterion for attribution holds the possibility of a type of enterprise liability in practice. This will never amount to an automatic tort liability merely by virtue of being part of a group. Such an automatic tort liability would go against the very idea of asset partitioning. But in an integrated group, it is possible to argue that an activity that wrongfully caused damages can be attributed to several entities of the group because of the broad substantive criterion for attributions. It would be required to demonstrate that the wrongful activity "is intrinsically linked with the pursuing of the objectives of other entities or the safeguarding of their interests or are perpetrated on their account based on the particular circumstance." The mere fact that formal elements associated with the tort point at one legal entity (*e.g.*, as the employer of the employees involved or as owner of the assets involved) should not be sufficient to get other legal entities off the hook.

So far we are not aware of Belgian case law that has explicitly applied this type of "enterprise liability" for torts or crimes.

4.3.2 Enterprise Liability in Competition Law

The "single economic entity" doctrine in EU and Belgian competition law can also be considered to be a type of "enterprise liability" looking at the economic reality of the group and disregarding the asset partitioning set up by the use of separate legal entities. According to case law of the European Court of Justice, parent companies can be fined for antitrust infringements by their subsidiaries; in addition, the amount of the fines will take the turnover of the economic entity into account. Belgian competition law follows this approach.

In the recent Vantaan kaupunki-case (C-724/17), the European Court of Justice included the application of this de-partitioning approach to private damages for infringements on competition law. While this case was more about "economic continuity" – de-partitioning the asset partitioning caused by the use of a successor company – than "economic entity," it can be expected that the case law on parental liability for competition fines will also be applied to damages caused by competition infringements.[37]

36 H. Hansmann & R. Squire, "External and Internal Asset Partitioning: Corporations and Their Subsidiaries, The Oxford Handbook of Corporate Law and Governance (Forthcoming)"; Yale Law & Economics Research Paper No. 535. Available at: https://ssrn.com/abstract=2733862, p. 24.

37 *See* M. Verhulst & J. Van Eetvelde, "The CJEU Vantaan kaupunki case: piercing the corporate veil via private enforcement of EU competition law," Available at: https://corporatefinancelab.org/2019/03/18/the-cjeu-vantaan-kaupunki-case-piercing-the-corporate-veil-via-private-enforcement-of-eu-competition-law, March 18, 2019.

4.4 Directors' Liability as a Remedial De-partitioning Technique

4.1 Directors' Liability in a Group Context

Limited liability stands firmly as a principle for shareholders, but in Belgian law it does not extend to directors. They are not automatically liable, but they are also not automatically immune for wrongdoings. Directors' liability allows the benefits of asset partitioning for shareholders, while offering a tailored remedy for the abuse of asset partitioning.

Directors' liability often amounts in fact to shareholders' liability. In a close corporation, the controlling shareholders will typically also be directors. In a subsidiary, the directors are often employees or agents of the parent company, which typically also indemnifies the directors from any liability. In both cases, the liability is likely to often shift through indemnification economically from the director to the controlling shareholder or parent company. This can be seen as a kind of remedial de-partitioning to the benefit of creditors.

In a public corporation, the distinction between the roles of directors and that of shareholders will be more sharply drawn. In particular, if the shareholders are dispersed, it will be unlikely that the directors will be indemnified.

Hence, directors' liability is likely to work differently in the case of internal asset partitioning (*e.g.*, close corporations and subsidiaries) and external asset partitioning (*e.g.*, public corporations). In the case of internal asset partitioning, it is more likely that directors' liability has a remedial de-partitioning effect.

This distinction follows the economic justifications for limited liability, which apply less to close corporations. It also mirrors the practice for strong contractual creditors, who, when confronted with a close corporation or subsidiary as counterparty, will bargain for a guarantee by the controlling shareholder(s). Such a guarantee is also a – selective – de-partitioning technique (see later). Directors' liability offers a similar result for other creditors (involuntary or non-adjusting creditors). Unlike a guarantee, directors' liability is a remedial de-partitioning technique based on a wrongdoing.

5 Directors' Liability and Corporate Interest Test as a Remedy against Selective De-partitioning

5.1 Statutory Limits to Selective De-partitioning

5.1.1 Corporate Interest Tests in a Group Context: The Rozenblum Doctrine

Although every transaction by a company should be justified in its best interests, Belgian company law allows group companies to make certain "sacrifices" in the common interest of the group, a legal theory known as the *Rozenblum* doctrine. In that way, Belgian company law (at least) to some extent recognizes the economic connection between organizations that are, legally speaking, entirely separate entities. Under certain conditions, Belgian company law thus recognizes that the group is more than a collection of separate companies.

The conditions of the *Rozenblum* doctrine, which are derived from a landmark judgment of the French Court of Cassation, can be summarized as follows:[38]

- the "sacrifice" of the relevant group member should be justified in the common interest of the group, taking into account the common group policies and objectives;
- the transaction should have at least some mutual consideration;
- there should be a *reasonable balance* between the respective liabilities of the group members; and
- the "sacrifice" should not exceed the *financial capacity* of the individual group member.

Therefore, a group company is allowed to transfer assets to another group member only if such transfer is made for at least some consideration, justified in the common interest of the group, compensated by other advantages and does not endanger the continuity of the relevant group member.

5.1.2 Belgian Tax Law Favors Internal Asset Partitioning

Belgian tax law is one of a handful of modern European tax systems that focuses primarily on separate entities and persons to establish the taxable base and levy taxes. Two examples:

- A single-shareholder company and the shareholder of such company will be taxed separately. As a principle, a legal person is not transparent from a tax perspective. The income of a single-shareholder company is taxed at the level of that company and not at the level of the shareholder; the shareholder gets taxed only on income that she gets from the company. This results in a widespread use of management companies with a single shareholder. Many directors of Belgian companies, for instance, are legal persons. This practice is driven not so much by a desire to enjoy the benefits of asset partitioning as by a desire to optimize the tax situation of the shareholder. The result is, however, an increased use of asset partitioning through single-shareholder companies (which we consider to be a type of internal asset partitioning).
- In a corporate group, the corporate income tax is assessed and levied at the level of the individual entities of the group and not at a consolidated level. This implies that the same business reality can, through the use of separate legal entities, be structured in many ways with different tax consequences. In practice, this gives an incentive for

38 *See* Cass. (FR) February 4, 1985, Rozenblum, *Bull Crime.* 1985, 145, n° 54. *See also* E. Wymeersch, "The law of groups of companies according to Belgian law," FLI working paper, 6-7.

internal asset partitioning through the use of subsidiaries and other affiliated companies.

5.1.3 Belgian Tax Law Enforces Prohibitions on Selective De-partitioning

The entity-driven approach of Belgian tax law implies that Belgian tax law and tax authorities are very much concerned about intragroup transactions that are not at arm's length.

Belgian tax laws have important provisions that tackle artificial profit shifting. The main example are the provisions on so-called abnormal or gratuitous benefits ("*abnormale of goedgunstige voordelen*").

These provisions have a severe punitive character. An abnormal or gratuitous benefit will be added to the taxable basis of the benefit's beneficiary. The benefit should be added back to the taxable income of the grantor as a disallowed expense unless the benefit was taken into account to determine the taxable basis of the beneficiary. Even if the abnormal or gratuitous benefit was taken into account to determine the taxable basis of the beneficiary, the benefit can be added (*e.g.*, as a disallowed expense) to the taxable basis of the grantor of the benefit. A benefit received from an affiliate cannot be offset by the beneficiary against its current or carried forward tax losses or other tax deductions.

As a consequence, Belgian tax law and the enforcement by tax authorities (which have dedicated transfer pricing investigation units) serve as an important safeguard against selective de-partitioning through shifting with assets and liabilities within a corporate group. While both company and tax lawyers will insist on the autonomy of their respective tests, the notion of "abnormal or gratuitous benefit" will in practice overlap with related-party transactions that fail a "corporate benefit" test. The tax authorities care more about asset-shifting than secured creditors who benefit from selective de-partitioning. The tax authorities have a stronger incentive to monitor intragroup relations than unsecured creditors (who suffer from rational apathy) and can use the full force of the tax investigation and enforcement apparatus. (Few other creditors have the right to force an unannounced "visit" upon their debtor).

5.2 *Directors' Liability and* Actio Pauliana *as a Remedy against Selective Departitioning through Guarantees*

5.2.1 Application: Personal Guarantees for the Liabilities of Affiliated Entities

As will be discussed in more detail, a company group structure allows the ultimately controlling shareholder to divide a single business between several legal entities. This division has a potential value-reducing effect for the creditor of a separate entity of the group, as the value of the assets of all legal entities combined – the "business"/"enterprise" as a whole – will often far exceed the aggregate value of the assets of the individual legal entities.

Professional lenders such as banks can bargain around this problem and typically require personal guarantees (apart from other security rights and liens) from all legal entities affiliated with the borrower. Such personal guarantees provide a double advantage to the lender in comparison with other creditors: not only does the lender receive all of the assets of multiple debtors as collateral for his debt, but he also benefits from a surplus value as a result of being able to sell a coherent set of assets (the business) as a whole.[39]

Moreover, should multiple guarantors go bankrupt, the lender is allowed to file a claim in each of the bankruptcy proceedings for the full nominal amount, until he is paid back entirely.[40]

Asset partitioning is a reality for involuntary creditors and other nonadjusting ("involuntary/voluntary") creditors, but rarely imposes itself on creditors with a strong bargaining position ("voluntary/voluntary creditors").

5.2.2 Corporate Interest Principle and *Actio Pauliana* against Personal Guarantees

In contrast to the case where key assets are (*ab initio*) divided between different legal entities (as set out later), it is rather easy for company creditors to demonstrate that the selective piercing of the corporate veil in favor of a lender by means of a personal guarantee negatively affects their right of recourse.

As a result of the guarantee, the company creditors are faced with an additional creditor with whom they will have to share the proceeds of their debtor's assets in case of default. If the outstanding liabilities of the debtor company exceed the total value of its assets, the creditors will obviously have to subsidize a larger part of the deficit than if there had been no guarantee.

Creditors (and trustees during a bankruptcy procedure) therefore regularly invoke the corporate interest principle and/or the *actio pauliana* to challenge personal guarantees and/or security rights provided by a company to secure a loan taken out by an affiliated company.

39 *See*, R. Squire, "Strategic Liability in the Corporate Group," *The University of Chicago Law Review*, 2011, p. 606 "*When a business firm gets big enough, it reliably does two things. First, it reconfigures itself into a corporate group by dividing itself into a multitude of commonly owned subsidiaries. Second, it causes the various entities in this group to guarantee each other's major outside debts.*"

40 *See* Art. XX.177 Belgian Code of Economic Law.

5.2.3 Guarantees and Reasonably Equivalent Value

The discussion typically hinges on whether the company providing the guarantee received reasonably equivalent value in consideration for this liability. In that respect, it is interesting to note that the mere fact that a company forms part of a corporate group does not constitute consideration as such under Belgian law.[41] Consequently, a transaction may be considered gratuitous even if entered into by a company in favor of an affiliate.

If the guarantee was indeed granted without reasonably equivalent value, the creditor will still need to establish that the absence of reasonably equivalent value cannot be justified by legitimate business considerations. If that is the case, the guarantee violates the corporate interest principle and/or is considered "fraudulent" for purposes of the *actio pauliana*, as set out earlier.

5.2.4 Gratuitous Guarantees and the *Rozenblum* Doctrine

As discussed, in the case of a group company, the question as to whether or not a transaction is justified in the corporate interest (and hence whether or not it is fraudulent for purposes of the *actio pauliana*) is answered on the basis of the so-called *Rozenblum* doctrine. In short, under that doctrine a group company is allowed to transfer value to an affiliate only if such transfer is made for at least some consideration, is justified in the common interest of the group, is compensated by other advantages, and does not endanger the continuity of the relevant group member.

Consequently, a guarantee without reasonably equivalent value may be compatible with the *Rozenblum* doctrine if the guarantor has received at least some consideration and indirectly benefits from the secured loan, even if such indirect benefits do not constitute consideration as such. For example, the proceeds of the secured loan may be used to finance an investment or research project of the borrower from which the guarantor will also benefit, be it indirectly and/or in the slightly longer term.[42]

For example, in a bankruptcy case before the Antwerp court of appeals, a guarantee agreement was challenged on the grounds of, *inter alia*, the *actio pauliana*. Taking into account all factual circumstances of the case, the court agreed with the defendants that the guarantee was justified in light of the common economic goal of the corporate group and hence dismissed the bankruptcy trustee's avoidance action.[43] Applying the same logic, the court of appeals of Liège held that a guarantee in favor of an affiliate is not

---

41 *See, e.g.,* K. Geens, M. Wyckaert, C. Clottens, F. Parrein, S. de Dier & S. Cools, "Overzicht van rechtspraak. Vennootschappen 1999-2010," *TPR*, 2012, (73) 149, para. 69; F. Jenné, "Zekerheden in groepsverband: een onzeker lot?" (annotation of Cass. September 30, 2005), *TRV*, 2006, pp. 593-595, para. 3; D. Napolitano, "Zekerheidsstelling in groepsverband – de bankier als jurist tegen wil en dank" (annotation of Cass. 9 March 2000), *TRV*, 2001, (96) 98, para. 7.

42 *See also* B. Lecourt, "De l'utilité de l'action paulienne en droit des sociétés," in L. Amiel-Cosme e.a., *Aspects actuels du droit des affaires: mélanges en l'honneur de Yves Guyon*, Paris, Dalloz, 2003, pp. 615-652, para. 84.

43 Court of Appeals of Antwerp October 7, 2004, *RABG* 2007, 45, annotation by S. Loosveld.

fraudulent for purposes of the *actio pauliana* insofar as it meets the requirements of the *Rozenblum* doctrine (without explicitly referring to it).[44]

5.2.5 More Stringent Rules on Gratuitous Guarantees during "Suspect Period"

The finding that the guarantee was provided without reasonably equivalent value is particularly important in the case that bankruptcy proceedings are opened against the guarantor and the guarantee was provided during the so-called "suspect period." This period comprises the time frame between the moment the debtor discontinued his payments and the time the bankruptcy proceedings opened. The exact period is determined by the bankruptcy judge and has a maximum duration of six months.[45]

Belgian bankruptcy law lists a number of transactions that a bankruptcy trustee may set aside when entered into by the debtor during the suspect period, regardless of whether the debtor acted with the intent or knowledge of harming his creditors.[46] Among others, the list includes all transactions entered into without reasonably equivalent value.[47] Thus, a guarantee provided without reasonably equivalent value during the suspect period can be avoided rather easily in a subsequent bankruptcy procedure, even if the purpose of the guarantee was to secure a loan received by an affiliated company in the common interest of the corporate group.[48]

44 Court of Appeals of Liège April 25, 1988, *JLMB* 1988, 1312. *See also* Comm. Liège October 13, 1981, *RPS* 1982, p. 45.

45 *See* Art. XX.105 of the Belgian Code of Economic Law. The maximum duration is subject to an exception in case the debtor company was already in liquidation prior to the cessation of payments and provided that there are indications that the liquidation is or was prompted by the intent to harm creditors.

46 *See also* I. Verougstraete, *Manuel de la continuité des entreprises et de la faillite,* Waterloo, Kluwer, 2011, p. 440, para. 3.3.7.1.

47 *See* Art. XX.111, 1° of the Belgian Code of Economic Law.

48 Cass. April 7, 2005, *Arr.Cass.* 2005, 794 (subsidiary in favor of parent); Cass. March 9, 2000, *Arr.Cass.* 2000, 550 (parent in favor of subsidiary). *See also* G. Lindemans, "Artikel XX.111-XX.114 WER" *in* H. Braeckmans, F. de Tandt, E. Dirix, T. Lysens & E. Van Camp (eds.), *Faillissement en Reorganisatie*, Mechelen, Kluwer, 2018, (7.B.1-1) 7.B.1-6, para. 12; K. Geens, M. Wyckaert, C. Clottens, F. Parrein, S. de Dier & S. Cools, "Overzicht van rechtspraak. Vennootschappen 1999-2010," *TPR*, 2012, (73) 146-147, para. 146; E. Dirix, "Zekerheden, eigendomsvoorbehoud en rangregeling," *in* H. Braeckmans, H. Cousy, E. Dirix, B. Tilleman & M. Vanmeenen (eds.), *Curatoren en vereffenaars: actuele ontwikkelingen*, Antwerp, Intersentia, 2006, pp. 519-552, para. 6; E. Van Camp & I. Mertens, *Nieuwe wetgeving. Faillissementswet anno 2008*, Mechelen, Kluwer, 2008, p. 94, para. 224; P. Ommeslaghe, "Les financements de groupe," *in* J.P. Buyle (ed.), *La banque dans la vie de l'entreprise*, Brussels, JBB, 2005, pp. 225-255, para. 22.

6 De-partitioning and Artificial Asset Partitioning in Insolvency Law

6.1 De-partitioning in the Insolvency of a Corporate Group

6.1.1 The Corporate Group in Belgian Insolvency Law

Like many other jurisdictions, Belgian insolvency law traditionally did not recognize the corporate group as such.[49] The fact that legal persons with corporate personality form part of a larger group was known but ignored.

Very recently, Belgian insolvency law has been reformed. Book XX of the Belgian Code of Economic Law contains the rules on insolvency and enterprises. Some of these rules are important for corporate groups. The first set of rules can be found in Article XX.13 and deals with matters of procedural coordination. The second rule can be found in Article XX.87 and deals with the so-called *auto-cession*.

6.1.2 Procedural Coordination

A distinction is generally made between procedural coordination and substantive consolidation. The *Uncitral Legislative Guide on Insolvency Law, Part three: Treatment of enterprise groups in insolvency* provides the following definition of both techniques of dealing with enterprise groups in insolvency law:

> - "Procedural coordination": coordination of the administration of two or more insolvency proceedings in respect of enterprise group members. Each of those members, including its assets and liabilities, remains separate and distinct.
> - Substantive consolidation": the treatment of the assets and liabilities of two or more enterprise group members as if they were part of a single insolvency estate.

The crucial distinction between procedural coordination and substantive consolidation deals with the respect that is given to the existing asset partitioning within the corporate group. Procedural coordination recognizes and respects the fact that each company group represents a separate bundle of assets (which serve as collateral for separate groups of creditors). At the same time, procedural coordination takes into account the fact that the group is more than just a collection of separate legal entities. Substantive consolidation, on the other hand, does not respect the legal separation between the corporate group

49 *See* in general, Report of the Review Committee, Insolvency Law and Practice (Cmmd. 8558, 1982) para. 1922: "*Group activity in the sense of the conduct of various businesses by a holding company through a number of subsidiaries is a Twentieth Century phenomenon. The principles of our company law and of our insolvency law were developed in the Nineteenth Century. It is not surprising, therefore, that some of the basic principles of company and insolvency law fit uneasily with the modern commercial realities of group enterprise.*"

members. The existing de-partitioning is discarded, and all assets are treated as being part of one estate.

The following table illustrates the difference in approach to group companies in insolvency. Traditional insolvency law ignores the group. Substantial consolidation ignores the group companies. Procedural coordination recognizes both the group and the group companies.

	Group companies	**Group**
Traditional insolvency law	X	0
Substantive consolidation	0	X
Procedural coordination	X	X

Substantive consolidation goes against the very foundations of asset partitioning. Indeed, what is the use of creating (and maintaining, with all the costs involved) a separation between group companies if such separation is totally ignored once the group companies enter into insolvency. That is why substantive consolidation should only rarely be applied (*e.g.*, in cases where it is impossible or too costly to separate the estates of the group companies).

Who would be the prime victim of substantive consolidation, shareholder or creditors? Clearly the latter. Imagine a situation whereby a voluntary/voluntary creditor (Justus) has negotiated a contract with company A, based on an expected return should company A become bankrupt. If company A is part of a company group (together with companies B and C) and if substantive consolidation is applied, Justus will have to share the assets of company A with the creditors of companies B and C. If company A has more assets than B and C, Justus runs the risk of receiving less after substantive consolidation than before substantive consolidation.

Unlike substantive consolidation, procedural coordination respects the boundaries of the separate estates of the group companies. Procedural coordination, and the techniques to achieve such coordination, looks beyond these boundaries, with the intention to capture the added value of the corporate group and to maintain this added value, also in the context of insolvency proceedings.

The general idea in favor of procedural coordination and against substantive consolidation is expressed as follows in recital 54 of the Insolvency Regulation (Recast):

> With a view to further improving the coordination of the insolvency proceedings of members of a group of companies, and to allow for a coordinated restructuring of the group, this Regulation should introduce procedural rules on the coordination of the insolvency proceedings of members of a group of companies. Such coordination should strive to ensure the efficiency of the coordi-

nation, whilst at the same time respecting each group member's separate legal personality.

6.1.3 Elements of Procedural Coordination in Belgian Law

Article XX. 13 contains two rules of procedural coordination. The first rule states that the court with jurisdiction (jurisdiction is confirmed on the basis of the well-known COMI-criterion) over an insolvency proceeding concerning a group company has jurisdiction over insolvency proceedings concerning other group companies. The second rule states that the competent court can assign a common insolvency practitioner for all proceedings.

The idea behind these rules is quite simple. Valuable information with respect to the group as a whole should be concentrated and not dispersed. By making one court competent for all group companies and one insolvency practitioner responsible for all proceedings, the going concern value of the group can be preserved.

6.2 Artificial Asset Partitioning Tackled in Insolvency Law

6.2.1 Artificial Asset Partitioning in the Vicinity of Insolvency

As mentioned before, a company group structure allows the ultimately controlling shareholder to divide assets and liabilities between several legal entities, although they are economically part of one and the same business. In the case that the insolvency of one of those entities is imminent, the corporate veil between them allows the controlling shareholder to opportunistically siphon off assets from the company in financial difficulties to other entities under his control.

As discussed earlier, transactions that frustrate the full recovery of a creditor's claim and that are deemed "abnormal" are voidable by means of the *actio pauliana* if the harmful effect was foreseeable at the time of the transaction.

An (almost) insolvent company arguably acts "abnormally" if it transfers certain assets to another legal entity while keeping assets that are, functionally or even physically, complementary to the transferred assets. Consequently, such a transfer is voidable if the harm to the creditors (in particular the debtor's insolvency) was reasonably foreseeable at the time of the transfer. This considerably limits the freedom of controlling shareholders to opportunistically spread key assets across group members in light of the insolvency of one or more of them.

6.2.2 Artificial Asset Partitioning *in Tempore Non Suspect*

The scope of application of the *actio pauliana* (and the corporate interest principle related to it) is, however, not limited to transfers in the twilight zone prior to insolvency. Creditors – or the bankruptcy trustee on their behalf – can also challenge transactions entered into at a time when the debtor company's insolvency was not yet reasonably foreseeable, provided that they cannot be justified in the best interests of the company.

As mentioned, such unjustified transfers may be voided on the grounds that they were prompted by the intent to harm creditors and/or violate the corporate interest principle. Unsurprisingly, the conditions of the aforementioned *Rozenblum* doctrine can also be found in the case law on the *actio pauliana* against intragroup transactions.[50]

6.2.3 Artificial Asset Partitioning at the Time of Incorporation: Harm Requirement as Achilles Heel

It follows from the foregoing that the corporate interest principle and the *actio pauliana* limit the freedom of controlling shareholders to opportunistically shift key assets from one legal entity to another without reasonable justification and/or in the twilight zone prior to insolvency.

However, both the corporate interest principle and the *actio pauliana* require showing of harm.[51] Indeed, a creditor bringing a claim for nullity, avoidance, or liability must prove that he is worse off as a result of the contested transaction than he would have been in the hypothetical case where the transaction never happened.[52]

This requirement is arguably the Achilles heel of those remedies in the case that complementary assets are not transferred to another entity during the company's "lifetime" but divided between multiple legal entities from the very beginning. In particular, a controlling shareholder may separate assets that are inextricably linked by contributing some of them to one company under his control while contributing others to another company.

In such a case, the creditors of the respective companies arguably suffer no harm as a result of the contribution. On the contrary, their debtor acquires assets in consideration for shares, which in principle only give entitlement to a subordinated claim on (a portion of) the company's profit. Because the creditors' claims have priority over the shareholders', they can arguably only benefit from a contribution. It can therefore be argued that a contribution of assets, even if they are artificially separated from other assets, can never harm the company's creditors.

6.2.3 Endowment Effect of Corporate Interest Principle and *Actio Pauliana*

Seen from the perspective of company creditors, one could thus say that the corporate interest principle and the *actio pauliana* suffer from a kind of "endowment effect," in that

50 *See* the case-law discussed in G. Lindemans, *Actio pauliana: een remedie met toekomst voor schuldeisers van rechtspersonen*, diss. KU Leuven, 2018, p. 292, para. 410.

51 *See also* S. De Dier, *Nietigheid van bestuursbesluiten in een vennootschap: inzichten op basis van een functionele benadering van de nietigheidssanctie*, Roeselare, Roularta, 2016, p. 329, para. 360.

52 *See also* G. Lindemans, *Actio pauliana: een remedie met toekomst voor schuldeisers van rechtspersonen*, diss. KU Leuven, 2018, p. 116, para. 150.

they only aim to safeguard (the value of) the assets the company has actually acquired. For example, the selective piercing of the corporate veil between various affiliates by means of personal guarantees is challengeable on the grounds of the corporate interest principle and/or the *actio pauliana*, as already discussed. By contrast, the fact that a company has received assets at the time of its incorporation that were separated from other assets in a value-reducing manner is in itself not a harmful event for which the company creditors can seek legal redress.

6.2.4 Statutory Rule on "Auto-Cession" as a Remedy against Artificial Asset Partitioning

One of the few specific statutory rules relevant for corporate groups deals with the so-called *auto-cession*. This rule applies only in the case of transfer of business in a judicial reorganization (though the problem could just as easily arise in the case of bankruptcy). A company enters into judicial reorganization proceedings with a view to transferring all or part of the business (asset deal). In return, the company receives money that is distributed to its creditors.

In practice, a bid is often made by insiders (shareholder and/or directors), who propose to buy all or part of their "own" business (*auto-cession*). Such an insider sale is forbidden in France (Art. L642-3 Code de Commerce) but allowed in Belgium.

The problem with such insider sales is that insiders have a strategic advantage over outsiders. First, they know a lot more about the business than outsiders. Secondly, their legal position may be stronger than that of third parties. Consider, for example, the situation where all the hardware is the property of company A but all IP rights are located in company B. Companies A and B have the same shareholders. Without access to the IP rights, the hardware in company A is worth nothing. Insiders bidding for the business of company A therefore enjoy a comparative advantage over outsiders. They can make a low offer because they hold the IP rights in a separate company. Ultimately, this may result in a lower price for creditors of company A. Indeed, insiders may refuse to make the IP rights available (hold out) to outsiders (at a reasonable price), thereby controlling the auction process. By strategically placing assets in different companies, insiders artificially partition assets in order to opportunistically extract value from the creditors in case of insolvency.

In order to counterbalance the strategic advantage of insiders, Article XX.87, § 2 contains the following rule (see full text of this provision in the Annex):

> In case a bid is made by persons who control the undertaking (or controlled it during six months prior to the initiation of the judicial reorganization) and who either directly or indirectly control any rights which are necessary to continue the activities, the offer can only be taken into account if such rights are made accessible to other bidders under the same terms and conditions.

The idea behind this rule is to create a level playing field between insiders and outsiders. Insiders who directly (in their own estate) or indirectly (through other legal entities) control rights that are necessary to continue the activities are obliged to make these rights accessible to other (outside) bidders under the same terms and conditions. In practice, rights held by insiders that are vital for the continuity of the business will therefore need to be valuated.

6.2.5 Same Problem Can Arise in Case of Sale to Third Party

The statutory rule on auto-cession applies only in the case of a bid by an insider and only in the case of a judicial reorganization (and not in the case of a bankruptcy with a sale of a business in a going concern).

However, insiders can also opportunistically use artificial asset partitioning in the case of a sale through a third party. A classic example is dividing the business into an entity for the operational activities and an entity with the real estate and making sure that the real estate company is insolvency remote. In the case that the real estate is essential for continuing the business (*e.g.*, a factory), a third party will be interested in purchasing the assets of the operational company only if it will also acquire the business of or the shares in the real estate company. The third party will in itself be indifferent to the allocation of the total purchase price to the separate entities. The shareholders, however, have a strong interest in allocating as much of the total purchase price as possible to the real estate company. They will ultimately benefit from these proceeds, whereas the proceeds allocated to the operational company in judicial reorganization will likely be eaten up by its creditors.

The provisions on auto-cession do not tackle this situation. An artificial disproportionate allocation of a purchase price to entities that are not in insolvency or reorganization can be considered to be a harmful transaction that can be challenged through the *actio pauliana* and/or liability of the parties involved.

6.3 Toward More Remedial De-partitioning in Insolvency Law: Saving the Going Concern Value of the Group for the Creditors of the Entities?

6.3.1 An Elevated Duty of Care for Directors and Shareholders in the Case of an Integrated Group?

In an integrated and interwoven group, it could be said that the going concern value of the business is a kind of "jointly owned asset" among the members of the group. One could even qualify the group as a silent partnership among the members of the group: the group as such does not contract with third parties, but internally they have an elevated duty akin to that of partners in a partnership.

Such an elevated duty is as such not to be found in Belgian case law, but one could make a credible argument that it exists as an application of existing rules on good faith, implied contracts, silent partnership, ... Even in the absence of any abuse of asset partitioning, remedial departitioning might be imposed because of closely interwoven group relations which are not illegitimate in itself.

Belgian law allows that the company engages in transactions that are, because of group benefits, only beneficial to the company in the long term; the corporate interest can, as discussed earlier, to an extent, be "colored" by the group interest. The existence of a going concern value transcending the separate entities is the justification for allowing selective de-partitioning.

The flip side of this doctrine, however, might be that courts tend to impose on the other entities of the group an elevated duty of care toward the company. When the group benefit is routinely invoked to justify certain transactions, this comes at a price when the company is in financial difficulties: then the "long-term" group benefit might translate into an elevated duty of care. The idea is that a shareholder cannot be allowed to invoke the benefits of limited liability when it did not respect the separate legal personality of the company. While less generally recognized, it might also be argued that if, in general, the interest of the company were ancillary to the interest of the group, there is an elevated duty of care, which imposes on the shareholders (or even other entities of the group) a duty to support the company to a certain extent.

An elevated duty of care will never amount to a blank duty to support the company at any cost under all circumstances. However, it could entail a duty to safeguard the common going concern value and to partition its value among the members of the group. The justification for allowing selective de-partitioning also suggests a more far-reaching rule on remedial de-partitioning in case of insolvency.

6.3.2 Inspiration from Rules on Secured Creditors in Insolvency?

A similar conflict exists in an insolvent business without asset partitioning but with secured creditors; security interests are, after all, similar to entity shielding as they allocate separate (pools of) assets to specific creditors. This creates a conflict between the secured creditors that are primarily interested by the liquidation value of their collateral and the other creditors that are primarily interested by the going concern value of the business as a whole.

The situation in a corporate group is similar, though not identical, in that creditors are interested by the value of the separate entity and that the execution of the assets of a separate entity might destroy the going concern value of the group.

Group insolvency law can perhaps look at the approach taken by the Belgian legislature toward secured creditors. Traditionally, a secured creditor enjoyed a very strong position in the bankruptcy of the debtor: as a "separatist," the secured creditor was not affected by the automatic stay and could execute even if such execution would destroy the going concern value of the business. Today, this strong position has been reduced in Belgian insolvency law. While the *value* of the collateral is still reserved for the secured creditor, he is restricted from taking unilateral action that could damage the (going concern) value of the bankruptcy estate. It is up to the bankruptcy trustee to sell the business as a going concern and then partition the proceeds with respect to the priority rights of the secured creditors (thus triggering difficult valuation issues).

Similarly, procedural coordination of the insolvency of a group could be conceived as an instrument to preserve the going concern value of the business at the group level. This would entail de-partitioning at the moment of the execution of the business of the individual group entities, while asset partitioning would be fully respected when the *value* of such sale would be divided over the individual entities and their creditors.

One could go even further and involve solvent entities of the group in such a consolidated procedure. This would effectively tackle artificial asset partitioning.

The interests of the group cannot be selectively invoked: if they are relevant in good times (to justify selective de-partitioning), they should also be in bad times (to justify remedial de-partitioning), and perhaps even beyond the point insolvency parts the entities of the group.

Annex - Article XX.87 § 2 of the Belgian Code on Economic Law (regarding the auction of assets in case a bid is made by a person controlling the debtor and who has rights which are necessary to continue the activities)

Dutch (official)	French (official)	English
§ 2. Ingeval een offerte uitgaat van personen die controle op de onderneming uitoefenen of hebben uitgeoefend gedurende zes maanden voorafgaand aan de opening van de procedure, en die rechtstreeks of onrechtstreeks de controle hebben over rechten die noodzakelijk zijn voor de voortzetting van haar activiteiten, kan die offerte slechts in aanmerking worden genomen op voorwaarde dat die rechten onder dezelfde voorwaarden toegankelijk zijn voor de andere bieders.	**§ 2.** Au cas où une offre émane de personnes qui exercent ou ont exercé le contrôle de l'entreprise pendant six mois avant l'ouverture de la procédure et exercent en même temps directement ou indirectement, le contrôle sur des droits nécessaires à la poursuite de ses activités, cette offre ne peut être prise en considération qu'à la condition que ces droits soient accessibles dans les mêmes conditions aux autres offrants.	**§ 2.** In case a bid is made by persons who control the undertaking (or controlled it during six months prior to the initiation of the judicial reorganization) and who either directly or indirectly control any rights which are necessary to continue the activities, the offer can only be taken into account if such rights are made accessible to other bidders under the same terms and conditions.

Dutch (official)	French (official)	English
§ 3. De kandidaat-bieder kan één of meer lopende overeenkomsten aanwijzen die niet intuitu personae zijn gesloten tussen de schuldenaar en één of meer medecontractanten die hij integraal wenst over te nemen met inbegrip van uitstaande schulden, indien zijn offerte wordt aanvaard. In dat geval zal, indien de verkoop doorgaat overeenkomstig artikel XX.90, de betrokken bieder van rechtswege in de plaats worden gesteld van de schuldenaar in de door hem aangewezen overeenkomsten, zonder dat de medecontractant zijn toestemming dient te verlenen. Uitstaande schulden voortvloeiend uit de aldus aangewezen overeenkomsten, die de koper ten laste neemt, worden niet beschouwd als onderdeel van de prijs bedoeld in paragraaf 1, derde lid.	**§ 3.** Le candidat offrant peut indiquer un ou plusieurs contrats en cours qui ne sont pas ceux conclus intuitu personae entre le débiteur et un ou plusieurs cocontractants qu'il souhaite reprendre intégralement, dettes du passé incluses, si son offre est acceptée. Dans ce cas, si la vente s'effectue conformément à l'article XX.90, l'offrant concerné sera subrogé de plein droit dans les droits du débiteur dans le ou les contrats qu'il a indiqués, sans que le cocontractant doive donner son consentement. Les dettes du passé découlant des contrats ainsi indiqués, pris en charge par l'acquéreur, ne sont pas considérées comme élément du prix au paragraphe 1er, alinéa 3.	**§ 3.** A bidder can indicate one or more agreements between the debtor and other parties, provided such agreements are not of an *intuitu personae* nature, which he wants to fully assume (including all debts due under such agreements) upon acceptance of his bid. In such case, upon the closing of such sale pursuant to Article XX.90, such bidder will step into the legal position of the debtor under the agreement or agreements which he indicated in the bid, without the need for the consent of the other party to such agreement. Any outstanding debts under such agreements assumed by the acquirer, shall not be deemed to be part of the price of the bid referred to in § 3 third sub-paragraph.
§ 4. De aangewezen gerechtsmandataris stelt een of meer ontwerpen van gelijktijdige of opeenvolgende verkopen op, met vermelding van de stappen die hij heeft ondernomen, de voorwaarden van de voorgenomen verkoop en de rechtvaardiging van zijn ontwerpen, en voegt hij voor elke verkoop een ontwerp van akte bij. Hij legt de ontwerpen in het register neer en deelt daarenboven zijn ontwerpen mee aan de gedelegeerd rechter en aan de schuldenaar en, bij verzoekschrift op tegenspraak, waarvan minstens acht dagen voor de zitting kennis wordt gegeven aan de schuldenaar, vraagt hij aan de rechtbank de machtiging om te kunnen overgaan tot de uitvoering van de verkoop.	**§ 4.** Le mandataire de justice désigné élabore un ou plusieurs projets de vente concomitants ou successifs, en y exposant ses diligences, les conditions de la vente projetée et la justification de ses projets et en y joignant, pour chaque vente, un projet d'acte. Il dépose ses projets dans le registre et communique en outre ses projets au juge délégué et au débiteur et, par requête contradictoire, notifiée au débiteur huit jours au moins avant l'audience, il demande au tribunal l'autorisation de procéder à l'exécution de la vente.	**§ 4.** The court appointed officer prepares one or more proposals for simultaneous or consecutive sales, indicating the steps he has undertaken, the terms and conditions of the proposed sale and the justification for his proposal, and adds a draft deed for each sale. He deposits his proposals in the Central Insolvency Register, sends them to the supervising judge and to the debtor, and with an application inter partes, of which the debtor is notified at least 8 days prior to the court day, requests the court the authorization to proceed with the execution of the sale.

Dutch (official)	French (official)	English
§ 5. De rechtbank neemt geen enkele offerte of offertewijziging na dat verzoekschrift in aanmerking.	**§ 5.** Aucune offre ou modification d'offre postérieure à cette requête ne peut être prise en considération par le tribunal.	**§ 5.** No bid or change to an existing bid can be taken into account by the court after such application.

Strategic Asset Partitioning under Dutch Law

Arpi Karapetian and Frank M.J. Verstijlen[*]

1 Introduction

Corporate structures are a challenging phenomenon in Dutch law. Group structures raise difficult questions in various fields of law. In the case law and the legal doctrine, topics such as the piercing of the corporate veil, conflicts of interests, and the right of inquiry have been largely addressed.[1] The economic reality within which a group operates as a unity is at odds with the legal reality of its constituent separate corporate personalities, and there are avenues within this field that remain to be explored.

An issue that illustrates this distinction is strategic asset partitioning in group structures. In contrast to the topics already mentioned, this area has barely been discussed in the literature. At first glance, the lack of attention to the topic could be explained by the fact that asset partitioning is at the very heart of group structures. Given that corporate structures aim to distribute business risk and that partitioning assets between different legal entities is a suitable means to achieve that end, asset partitioning is arguably inherent to any legal system in which corporate personalities are acknowledged by law.

However, asset partitioning might be less harmless than it seems: other interests such as those of creditors and the public interest of the rescue of viable businesses can be harmed as a result of a prior strategic division of assets, particularly in the event of an insolvency.

In such cases, the question arises as to whether and to what extent Dutch law sets limits to such conduct. Strategic asset partitioning can manifest itself in different ways. Common types of asset partitioning are (i) establishing a corporate structure to divide the loss-making and profitable parts of a business into separate companies and (ii) assigning key assets such as intellectual property rights and real estate to other group companies than the operating company that uses these assets in the business.

In this report, we will address the aforementioned question in Dutch law in view of these two types of strategic asset partitioning. The first part of the report will focus on the consequences of asset partitioning on the options for recourse that creditors retain. We

* Dr. A. Karapetian is Assistant Professor in Private Law at the University of Groningen and prof. dr. F.M.J. Verstijlen is Professor of Private Law at the University of Groningen.

1 *See* S.M. Bartman, "De Hoge Raad weet zich niet goed raad met het concern," *Ondernemingsrecht*, 2016/77.

will discuss the case law of the Dutch Supreme Court concerning the liability of parties involved in asset partitioning. In the second part, we will pay attention to the suppression of value in insolvency resulting from strategic asset partitioning. Insolvency practitioners can encounter difficulties in maximizing the value recovered for creditors, particularly when trying to sell a business if key assets belong to other group companies.

2 Impairing Recourse Opportunities for Creditors

2.1 *Tort and* verhaalsbenadeling

In this section, we examine two cases in which the division of assets between different legal entities was deemed prejudicial to creditors. In both cases, the parties related to the debtor company were held liable for the creditors' loss on the basis of tortious behavior toward the creditors. The statutory basis for a claim in these situations is Article 162 of Book 6 *Burgerlijk Wetboek*. Pursuant to this article, torts can be divided into three categories: (i) violation of a right, (ii) breach of a statutory duty, and (iii) breach of a non-statutory duty stemming from the standard of due care. In the cases examined here, liability was based on the third category of tort.

The loss that the creditors suffered in these cases amounted to *verhaalsbenadeling*. *Verhaalsbenadeling* is best understood as a loss to creditors consisting of the erosion of the pool of assets against which creditors may take recourse. In typical cases concerning *verhaalsbenadeling*, the prejudicial behavior at issue occurred in the vicinity of insolvency. This can be explained by one of the requirements for liability. To establish liability, the standard requirement is that the tortfeasor could foresee that the debtor company would not meet its debts and would not offer recourse.[2]

If insolvency practitioners wish to rely on provisions pertaining to transaction avoidance (*actio Pauliana*) instead of bringing a liability claim, they will encounter a similar requirement. Pursuant to Article 42 *Faillissementswet*, a legal act (*rechtshandeling*) that was not legally compelled can be challenged if both the debtor and the counterparty knew or should have known that this would be prejudicial to the creditors. The Dutch Supreme Court redefined how knowledge of prejudice to the creditors is established in the landmark case *ABN AMRO/Van Dooren III*.[3] According to the Dutch Supreme Court, the test is whether "at the time of the occurrence of the act at issue the opening of an insolvency procedure and a deficit were reasonably foreseeable" for the debtor and the other contracting party. Consequently, if the disputed acts took place too long before this point, the *actio Pauliana* will be of no use to the joint creditors.

2 *Ibada Jelgersma*, HR February 19, 1988, NJ 1988/487, *Ontvanger/Roelofsen*, HR December 8, 2006, NJ 2006/659 and *Sobi/Hurks II*, HR December 21, 2001, NJ 2005/96.

3 HR December 22, 2009, NJ 2010/273.

Furthermore, since the *actio Pauliana* aims to challenge certain transactions between the debtor and the third parties, it will not be available in the event that the assets at issue never belonged to the debtor. This will, for instance, be the case when the assets were assigned to another company within a group from the outset.

The Dutch Supreme Court has in two cases held parties affiliated with a debtor liable for the loss that creditors suffered, without finding it necessary to indicate a reference date for the debtor's state of insolvency for the assessment of liability. The foreseeability of the debtor's insolvency was not a decisive legal issue in these cases. Liability was based on the corporate asset structure, of which the debtor was a part. Subsequently, these two cases constrain strategic asset division to a certain extent, from the perspective of due care.

The first case discussed here is *Comsys/Van den End q.q.*[4]

2.2 Comsys/Van den End q.q.

Comsys was a group comprising Comsys Holding, Comsys Services, and Comsys. The holding company acted as the sole director and shareholder of the two subsidiaries. The group was structured in such a way that Comsys Services dealt with the procurement and installation of products, while Comsys was assigned the concluding of contracts with counterparties and debt recovery. Comsys Services did not recover its costs completely for the products and services that it provided to Comsys. All the assets of Comsys Services were collateral for the money that the bank had lent to the group. Essentially, this corporate structure enabled a single enterprise to be conducted where Comsys Services operated at a loss from the outset and Comsys realized the profits.

Eventually, despite Comsys Services' significant losses, its accountant continued to value its assets on a going-concern basis following the express intention of the parent company to continue the business. The parent company was by that time aware that the continuation of Comsys Services depended on intracompany funding. The losses that Comsys Services bore were compensated in its current accounts within the group for a certain period. This current account offsetting was ended approximately three years after the aforementioned structure was established. As a result, Comsys Services filed a petition for bankruptcy, and the creditors were unable to recover.

The insolvency practitioner brought a liability claim against the parent company for recovery of the loss to the creditors consisting of the deficit in the bankruptcy estate.

The Court of Appeal allowed the claim against the parent company on the basis of Article 162 of Book 6 *Burgerlijk Wetboek*. It ruled that, in the aforementioned circumstances, the parent company owed a duty to the creditors of Comsys Services. In support of the imposition of this duty, it first referred to the close corporate connection between

4 HR September 11, 2009, NJ 2009/565 with annotation by H.J. Snijders & P. van Schilfgaarde.

the companies within the group, since they essentially conducted a single enterprise. It then determined that Comsys Services was entirely dependent in terms of financing on its parent company and the other subsidiary. Thirdly, the Court established that the parent company knew that Comsys Services' creditors might be prejudiced as a result of its conduct, given also that the parent company had previously expressed its intention to continue the activities of Comsys Services. Since the holding company had not warned the creditors, the Court ruled that it had breached its duty to the creditors when it decided to end funding through current account transfers to the detriment of the creditors and to file for insolvency.

In his opinion, the Advocate General L. Timmerman argued that establishing a corporate structure consisting of loss-making and profit-making subsidiaries is not tortious in itself. According to the Advocate General, such a structure, which inevitably entails risks for the creditors of the loss-making subsidiary, only amounts to a tort under Article 162 of Book 6 *Burgerlijk Wetboek* if the parent company does not act with due care. For this to be established, the court needs to designate a date on which the duty of the parent company to the creditors is activated. Only after that date can the parent company be held to a duty to warn the creditors, or in some other way to have regard for the interests of the creditors.

The Dutch Supreme Court did not follow the Advocate General's reasoning. It upheld the ruling of the Court of Appeal and did so considering the overall corporate structure that was established from the outset. At paragraph 5.2.1, the Dutch Supreme Court noted that the parent company's liability in this case was based on the fact that the parent company had created a corporate structure with inherent risks for the creditors of Comsys Services from the very beginning, which risks were amplified by the fact that the assets of Comsys Services served as collateral for the group's credit arrangement with the bank. The Court noted that despite the significant risks to the creditors, the parent company did not warn them and, while knowing that the continuation of Comsys Services was solely dependent on the internal financing, it did not take any other measures to mitigate those risks. Instead, it ended the current account with Comsys Services and filed for insolvency. In addition to this reasoning, the Dutch Supreme Court noted that in order to establish a breach of duty by the parent company, it is not necessary to determine a date of reference (*peildatum*).

Legal scholars have cautioned against deriving a general rule from this case.[5] According to them, the ruling focuses largely on the specific circumstances of the case. Moreover, the Dutch Supreme Court left room for the Court of Appeal when referring to the

5 Annotation P. van Schilfgaarde in NJ 2009/565, M.L. Lennarts, "HR September 11, 2009, LJN BH4033, NJ 2009, 565, m.nt. P. van Schilfgaarde, RO 2009, 67, RI 2009, 78, JOR 2009/309, m.nt. Spinath (Comsys/Van den End q.q.)," *Tijdschrift voor Insolventierecht* 2010, 24.

fact that the parent company was not sufficiently opposed to the prepositions of the insolvency practitioner.[6]

Beyond these reservations, *Comsys/Van den End q.q.* is considered an unusual case because the courts did not apply a reference date for the purposes of assessing the debtor's liability toward its creditors. The ruling was founded on the corporate structure, which was deemed to entail high risks for the creditors of the subsidiary. The corporate structure was particularly potentially harmful for the creditors of Comsys Services because Comsys Services was not paid in full or at all for the products and services it provided for the holding company and the other subsidiary.

It has been argued that the duty of the parent company in this case rests on maintaining a corporate structure within which intercompany dealings are not at arm's length.[7] In other words, it is a structure that includes a loss-making and a profitable company that together run as a single enterprise, which imposes a duty on the parent company to take its creditors' interests into account from the outset.[8] This reasoning could be taken a step further to suggest that the creation of the structure itself constitutes negligence, as it diverts the assets—*i.e.*, options for recourse—generated by the loss-making company to the group company, making these unavailable to the creditors of the loss-making company.[9] If a Comsys-like structure had not been established from the beginning but was imposed in the course of business, this would have also constituted a tort to the creditors. In other words, a holding company would incur liabilities not only to its future creditors but also to current creditors by changing its business structure to a Comsys-like one.

It has been argued that having regard to the creditors' interests means, in particular, that a parent company should notify its creditors about the risks—which would clearly not have supported the continuation of the loss-making company—or make sure that creditors receive payment.[10] Insofar as the liability extends to the creditors together—in *Comsys* the insolvency practitioner instituted a claim on behalf of the creditors collectively—such a warning is of no avail, because it would correct the unlawful nature of the parent's behavior vis-à-vis the individual creditors. However, the position of the tortfeasor vis-à-vis the individual creditors was not taken into account in the claim on behalf of

6 Lennarts 2010. *Cf.* N. Pelletier, La responsabilité au sein des groups de sociétés en cas de procedure collective, diss. 2013, nr. 179.

7 *Id.*

8 B.F. Assink/W.J. Slagter, *Compendium Ondernemingsrecht* (Deel 2), Deventer, Kluwer, 2012, p. 2275.

9 *Cf.* P.S. Bakker & I. Wassenaar, "Comsys: doorbraak zonder peildatum," Tijdschrift voor de Ondernemingspraktijk, 2010, p. 28, who argue that the structure itself constitutes negligence, although the parent's paying of the creditors eliminated its "negligent character" for a while. The parent's paying of the creditors through current account transfers can also be considered to be a damage prevention step. Even if approached in this way, the structure's negligent nature nonetheless persists throughout its trading.

10 P.S. Bakker & I. Wassenaar, "Comsys: doorbraak zonder peildatum," Tijdschrift voor de *Ondernemingspraktijk*, 2010, No. 1, p. 27.

the joint creditors.[11] A warning, moreover, would not have made sense—or even have been possible—for involuntary creditors such as those with claims arising from tort.

Incidentally, in the case law of the lower courts, insolvency practitioners have argued for recovery of losses to creditors of the parent company and/or the director of the bankrupt company on the basis of the *Comsys* ruling,[12] but the claims were dismissed in all cases. For instance, in 2015 the Court of Appeal held that despite the risks that the corporate structure in question entailed for the creditors, the parent company was not liable because the group's enterprise was not divided between a loss-making and a profitable company.[13] In this case, the debtor company's activities were closely connected to another group subsidiary's enterprise. The first instance court had established that the continuation of the debtor company was entirely dependent on intragroup financing. It was clear to all the parties involved that the debtor company would not survive if the intragroup funding was terminated. While the Court of Appeal adopted the lower court's view that this *modus operandi* implied risks to the creditors, it ruled that the *Comsys* rule could not apply because the debtor company did not bear the entire costs in the business while the other subsidiaries extracted its profits.[14]

This Court of Appeal ruling demonstrates the reluctance of the Dutch courts to restrain the principle of free enterprise and entrepreneurs' freedom to establish corporate structures as they please.[15] There is no rule in Dutch law that prohibits corporate structures that expose one group company's creditors to greater risks of no recovery than the creditors of other group companies.[16]

It has been argued that tax law could provide good reasons for such a course of conduct.[17] Based on the *Comsys/Van den End q.q.* judgment and the few lower court cases, it seems legitimate to state that a risky corporate structure establishes liability in tort for the parent company only when the group actually runs a single enterprise within which one subsidiary bears the costs of production and the other group companies receive the prof-

11 *Notarissen THB II*, HR December 23, 1994, NJ 1996/628.

12 Court of Appeal Arnhem-Leeuwarden January 13, 2015, ECLI:NL:GHARL:2015:203; District Court Amsterdam July 29, 2015, ECLI:NL:RBAMS:2015:6178. In the following case, the liability claim was submitted by a creditor: District Court Rotterdam January 6, 2016, ECLI:NL:RBROT:2016:248.

13 Court of Appeal Arnhem-Leeuwarden January 13, 2015, ECLI:NL:GHARL:2015:203.

14 *See* consideration 5.20 in the mentioned case.

15 *See*, for instance, Bartman 2010, point 6 in his annotation of *Comsys/Van den End q.q.* in Ars Aequi 2010/February.

16 Opinion of the Advocate General, paras. 3.2.3 and 3.3.2.

17 Bartman, 2010.

its, without paying the cost-incurring subsidiary in full or at all for the products and services it provides within the group.[18] In that case, where the debtor company operates at a loss and the parent company chooses to continue the business, it is under a duty to take into account the interests of the creditors of that company. Liability emerges, in other words, from a corporate structure that entails disproportionate risks to creditors —and rightly so, in our view. The loss-making company should at least receive reasonable compensation for the costs it incurs for the purposes of the enterprise.

It is not necessary to establish that the parent company had the intention to prejudice the creditors. It apparently suffices to argue that by establishing and maintaining such a structure, the parent company accepts the risks to the creditors and incurs liability when the risks materialize.

In contrast, the second case to be discussed here—*Stichting Waaldijk/Aerts q.q.*—appears to have required the intention of keeping assets beyond the reach of creditors for the finding of liability.[19]

2.3 Stichting Waaldijk/Aerts q.q.

X, a bankrupt, lived in a house, the use of which he fully enjoyed without being its legal owner. As a result, X's creditors could not take recourse against that property. The house belonged to a foundation, Stichting Waaldijk, that had been established by the bankrupt. The foundation's articles stated that it was established with the purpose of preserving monuments within the meaning of the *Monumentenwet* 1988 (a statute pertaining to the conservation of national monuments), and, in particular, to obtain the house that later became involved in the case. The legal ownership of the house was directly transferred to this foundation by its vendor. Immediately afterward, the economic ownership of the house was transferred to X. Stichting Waaldijk did not conduct business activities.[20]

Several years later, X established another foundation with the purpose of maintaining economic ownership of the house, which he transferred to this foundation. At the time of

18 *Cf.* consideration 4.17 of the District Court of Rotterdam in the already referred case ECLI:NL:RBROT:2016:248: "Dat het concern waartoe [failliete vennootschap] behoorde werken heeft laten aannemen door andere vennootschappen dan [failliete vennootschap] waarna het concern de werkzaamheden heeft laten uitvoeren door [failliete vennootschap], levert niet een gang van zaken op waarmee enige norm is overtreden. Deze werkwijze is binnen een concern niet ongebruikelijk. *Waar het om gaat is dat eventuele verrekeningen tussen verschillende van het concern deel uitmakende vennootschappen op zakelijke basis plaatsvinden* (authors' italics)." The sentence in italics points out that the Court attaches importance to intragroup transactions being at arm's length.

19 HR February 27, 2009, NJ 2009/318.

20 The insolvency practitioner argued that the costs of maintaining the house were borne by other companies for which person X acted as de facto director and that were eventually declared bankrupt. *See* para. 4.8 in the Court of Appeal's judgment.

the transfers, he was the director of both the foundation that had the legal ownership of the house and the foundation that held its economic ownership.

At some point, X was declared bankrupt. The insolvency practitioner brought liability claims against the foundation with the legal ownership of the house. The claim was based on the tort of negligence (Art. 162 of Book 6 *Burgerlijk Wetboek*) and concerned the losses incurred by the creditors. The insolvency practitioner argued that the foundation had not acted with due care by cooperating with the construction of the aforementioned ownership structure and maintaining it with the sole purpose of keeping the house out of reach of X's creditors in the event of bankruptcy.

The Dutch Supreme Court upheld the Court of Appeal's ruling and found the defendant liable. As a starting point, it ruled that if a person controls two companies, he is able to abuse the different corporate personalities of these companies and his own private personality. Such abuse can constitute a tort in negligence and will amount to liability for the loss that it creates for third parties. The liability concerns not only the person who caused those companies to commit a tort, but also the companies themselves, since, according to the Supreme Court, the wrongful intention – the abuse – should be attributed to these companies. In this case, the Court ruled that the wrongful intention consisted of placing the house out of X's ownership without serving any independent interest of the involved foundations and with the exclusive intention of prejudicing X's creditors. Contrary to what the defendant argued, this judgment held that it is not a prerequisite for finding liability that the asset in question should have once belonged to the person whose creditors were prejudiced.

The ruling offers an example of asset partitioning that was found to have been unlawful under Dutch law. In our view, the courts were persuaded to establish liability, in particular by the intentional undermining of the interests of the creditors. The parties' intention to deprive X's creditors of recourse could be derived from the ownership structure that was established. This structure served no economic objective but to impede the creditors' opportunities for recourse. There was no evidence of any intention to distribute the operational risks of an enterprise at issue.

The Dutch Supreme Court recently ruled in a similar manner in *Resort of the World/ Maple Leaf*.[21]

2.4 *Resort of the World/Maple Leaf*

Resort of the World was a public limited company under Sint Maarten law that operated a hotel. M had been working for this company as a financial controller for many years. A company related to Resort of the World embarked on a project that concerned the construction of villas. As part of this project, M expressed his intention to purchase a villa.

21 HR October 7, 2016, NJ 2017/124 with annotation by P. van Schilfgaarde.

M was the buyer of a villa in the relevant purchase agreement, for an amount favorable to M. Later, M established a foundation called Maple Leaf. It was established under Sint Maarten law with a coworker of M's as its director. According to its articles, the foundation was established for "the management of the capital, which has been set aside and earmarked for the benefit of the natural persons and legal entities and their relatives left behind, as well as charities designated by the Board and to pay distributions to above referred natural person(s) and legal entities and their relatives left behind, as well as charities."[22] M transferred the villa to Maple Leaf. M and his wife had lived in the villa for a period. For tax purposes, M considered the villa to be his property, and he covered the total costs of its maintenance. At a certain point, Resort of the World fired M with immediate effect for alleged fraud. It submitted a liability claim against M for damages flowing from the fraud. In addition, it brought a claim against Maple Leaf on several grounds, including liability for tortious curtailment of M's creditors' means of redress, and, in particular, for Resort of the World's fraud claim.

The Joint Court of Justice dismissed the defendant's argument that assigning the villa to the foundation was in accordance with statute, according to which private foundations can be established with the precise goal of separating assets.[23] It also agreed with M's argument that the structure in question was legitimate from the perspective of taxation.

This reasoning was set aside by the Dutch Supreme Court. Firstly, it ruled that the identification (*vereenzelviging*) of M with Maple Leaf went too far to establish a means of redress.[24] In its relevant explanation, the Court referred to the *Rainbow* case,[25] where the Supreme Court had decided that when a legal or natural person who has complete control of several legal entities misuses the difference in identity between the entities, under exceptional circumstances the identification of the various legal entities will be the most suitable means of relief. This implies that the separate identities of the parties involved will be disregarded in law and that the legal obligations, behavior, and knowledge of a

22 As stated in para. 3.1 in this Dutch Supreme Court ruling.

23 This can be found in para. 2.9 in this Dutch Supreme Court ruling. *See* paras. 4.9-4.15 of the opinion of the Advocate General T. Hartlief for an explanation of the Sint Maarten law on private foundations.

24 *See* paras. 3.5.2 and 3.5.3.

25 HR October 13, 2000, NJ 2000/698 with annotation by J.M.M. Maeijer.

particular legal or natural person will be attributed to another legal or natural person. The Court in *Rainbow*, however, did not apply this identification remedy. It reasoned that it could not be excluded that the recourse damages were less than the amount of the debt for which recourse was made impossible as a result of the exploitation of the legal entities. In the event of identification, the prejudiced creditor could be enabled to recover his entire debt – instead of the recourse damages only – and this potential effect was not accepted by the Court.

The Dutch Supreme Court has not applied the identification doctrine since *Rainbow*.[26] It has been argued that identification is an *ultimum remedium* and that in case of recourse damages, the tort of negligence (Art. 162 of Book 6 *Burgerlijk Wetboek*) constitutes an appropriate tool to compensate for damages.[27]

In *Maple Leaf*, the Supreme Court maintained its reservations about identification as a means of redress. As already mentioned, it decided that identifying M with Maple Leaf as a means of redress was a stretch too far.[28] However, it decided that in view of the facts and the circumstances in this case, the dismissal of the claim on the basis of the creditors' negligence would be incomprehensible. The Court, then, summed up the relevant facts established by the appellate court.[29] It highlighted that the villa was transferred to Maple Leaf without payment at a time when M should have been aware of and acting on the understanding that his fraud would be revealed and that this would lead to a claim from Resort of the World for a significant amount. In addition, the Court noted that M had paid the maintenance costs for this villa during the entire period and referred to the argument made by Resort of the World that M continued his fraud in the belief that the villa would be safe from recourse measures. Since M was in complete control of Maple Leaf – without, however, being its statutory director consistently – his actions can be attributed to the latter.[30] The Supreme Court eventually referred the case back to the Joint Court of Justice for review.

---

26 The Dutch Supreme Court accepted identification in an earlier case, *Krijger/Citco* (HR June 9, 1995, NJ 1996/213). The case concerned an authority for Citco Bank to serve a garnishee order on Krijger for debts owed to Lorimar. Krijger and Lorimar had concluded a contract for the construction of a house by Lorimar. Immediately after the garnishment, Krijger ended its contract with Lorimar and concluded a new contract with Intervorm. Intervorm had the same owner and director as Lorimar, and the construction of the house was continued with the same employees and the same building materials as those used by Lorimar. Moreover, Intervorm's Articles of Association were expanded to include "building activities" just a week before the garnishment was carried out. The Supreme Court accepted identification of Lorimar and Intervorm in this case, since it reasoned that the ending of one contract and the conclusion of the new contract were conducted with the sole purpose of avoiding Krijger's remaining debts under the building contract being caught by the garnishment order. For a lower court case in which the identification doctrine was applied, *see* District Court Zwolle July 24, 2002, ECLI:NL:RBZWO:2002:AF3673.

27 L. Timmerman, "Vereenzelviging als strijdmiddel in vennootschapsrechtelijke aansprakelijkheidsprocedures," Ondernemingsrecht 2001/10. *Cf.* M.L. Lennarts, annotation of *Rainbow* in *Ondernemingsrecht* 2000/54.

28 *See*, however, S.M. Bartman's critique of this part of the ruling in *Ondernemingsrecht* 2017/7.

29 Para. 3.6.2.

30 Para. 3.7.2.

As we have already mentioned, this case resembles *Stichting Waaldijk/Aerts q.q.* It is therefore somehow unclear why the Dutch Supreme Court did not refer to the latter case. These similarities were pointed out in the legal literature and in the opinion of the Advocate General T. Hartlief.[31] The key issue was that the allocation of assets was not (or not clearly) conducted for sound business reasons and the legal state of affairs did not correspond with the factual and economic situation.[32] On the basis of these precedents we would argue that in the event that assets have been allocated between different entities, this can constitute a tort if it is predominantly aimed at prejudicing creditors in the event that they need to take recourse. The wrongful intention can be derived from similar circumstances to those found in the aforementioned cases. The most relevant circumstances are that no sound business reasons can be provided for the separation of assets; that the person or entity entitled to the use and other benefits of the asset – such as the surplus value in the event of its sale – is not its legal owner; and that the entity that holds the legal title does not have an independent interest in the asset at issue.[33]

3 Suppressing Value Following from Asset Partitioning

3.1 Party Autonomy

We will now consider the situation whereby assets are distributed between the companies in a group in such a manner that the value of one of the group companies' assets can be completely realized only in combination with the assets of one or more other group companies.

Corporate structures often have this effect. Intellectual property rights, real estate, or even inventory can be held by one company, while the actual business is run by a different group company. If the latter company becomes insolvent, it may be all but impossible for the insolvency practitioner to continue or to sell the business if he cannot dispose of or at least have access to the assets of the other group companies.

Does Dutch law set limits to such corporate structures? The issue has barely been discussed in the Dutch literature, and there is no case law on the subject. However, we believe that Dutch law leaves considerable room for such structures.

The starting point is that according to the main principles of private law, parties are free to organize their affairs as they please, as a matter of party autonomy. This applies both to the separate legal entities and the structure of the group as such. There is no duty

31 Opinion of the Advocate General, para. 4.21; Bartman 2017; Annotation P. van Schilfgaarde in NJ 2017/124.

32 Elbers argues that this is a relevant aspect in finding liability on the basis of abuse of different corporate personalities. J. Elbers, *Misbruik van het identiteitsverschil en crediteursbenadeling* (diss.), Zutphen, Paris, 2014, nr. 3.2.

33 *See* Elbers, 2014, pp. 52-53.

on the separate companies to "own" the assets that they use in their business. There is no duty on the group companies and the parent company to divide the assets in such a way as to maximize the value of the assets of any particular group company.

There can be good reason to separate assets from the business risks of particular companies.[34] In fact, it is a, if not *the, raison d'être* for groups as such.

No one would expect a local McDonald's restaurant to actually own the McDonald's trademarks it uses, regardless of whether it is a franchise or a company-operated restaurant. These trademarks are vital for the global business and cannot be exposed to the insolvency risk of any particular restaurant. The same applies at the smallest scale. A baker who chooses to run his one-man bakery from a company could choose to transfer the ownership of the building out of which he runs his business to a separate real estate company to prevent his life savings from being lost if the business fails. He is free to do so.

3.2 *"Locking in" of the Business and the Goodwill*

There *are* limits to this freedom, which follow from the same principles as discussed in the previous section. There is, as already noted, no duty to maximize the value of any particular group company, but there is a duty not to impair the opportunities for the general body of creditors to have recourse for their claims.

If assets are distributed between companies with a view to ensuring that the total value – including surplus value, the goodwill – will not be available to creditors but can only be realized by an affiliated company,[35] this could constitute a negligence toward the general body of creditors. Hummelen offers the example of "earmarked assets," where pizza boxes bear a pizza chain's logo or clothes have a print of their designer's logo, as part of a predesigned scheme to acquire such assets at a depressed price.[36] He states that this behavior can be assumed in cases of repeat conduct, for instance if a pizza chain continuously has pizza shops established that go bankrupt, and from which it then buys the assets at a depressed price.

34 *Cf.* N. Pelletier, La responsabilité au sein des groups de sociétés en cas de procedure collective, diss. 2013, nr. 32 and 38.

35 This can also be regarded as an "instrumentalisation de la procedure collective par le groupe de sociétés." See N. Pelletier, La responsabilité au sein des groups de sociétés en cas de procedure collective, diss. 2013, nr. 10. However, it should be noted that in France, the opportunities for making use of insolvency proceedings in this manner are restricted by the exclusion of connected parties from the bidding process. *See* Art. 642-3 of the French Commercial Code, the first sentence of which reads: "Ni le débiteur, au titre de l'un quelconque de ses patrimoines, ni les dirigeants de droit ou de fait de la personne morale en liquidation judiciaire, ni les parents ou alliés jusqu'au deuxième degré inclusivement de ces dirigeants ou du débiteur personne physique, ni les personnes ayant ou ayant eu la qualité de contrôleur au cours de la procédure ne sont admis, directement ou par personne interposée, à présenter une offre." This is because "la cession ne doit pas être un moyen commode pour le débiteur de poursuivre l'activité sans le passif antérieur [...]" (André Jacquemont, Régis Vabres, Thomas Mastrullo, *Droit des entreprises en difficulté*, 2017, nr. 881).

36 J.M. Hummelen, *Distress dynamics*, diss. 2015, pp. 160-161.

In this case, the value of the "earmarked assets" themselves is depreciated – at least for the debtor entity and anyone else without the trademark or a license to use it – while the value of the individual assets might be unimpaired but the surplus value in the totality of the assets is, as it were, "earmarked." This also occurs when a patent or a bespoke machine that is crucial for a production process is owned by an affiliated company.[37]

Such a separation of key assets from a business can result in liability being found, regardless of whether the transaction that extracts the key asset in itself is detrimental as such, in the sense that it is transferred for the actual value actually paid and made available to the creditors. Consider, for instance, a case where a patent or crucial machine is transferred to an affiliated company for its actual value according to an official appraisal. It is not the value of the particular asset itself that is the problem in these cases, but the fact that the transaction "locks" the business and the insolvent company's goodwill – the surplus value a company is worth above its individual assets – to the owner of the transferred asset.

If the transfer of the key asset occurs when there is a reasonable expectation that the transferor will be the object of insolvency proceedings, the transfer is likely to be avoidable on the basis of the *actio Pauliana*. However, even when the transfer occurred long before insolvency was in sight and the transaction cannot be avoided,[38] group company liability can exist. The Dutch Supreme Court has decided that the provisions on transaction avoidance contain rules on what is allowed as between creditors and debtors, and that a transaction that is allowed by these provisions cannot be the target of a negligence action, unless there are special circumstances.[39] However, we would argue that the fact that the transaction was done with the aim of "locking" the business and the goodwill to the acquiring group company is a special circumstance that merits group company liability.

Moreover, the *actio Pauliana* is concerned with the detrimental effects of a transaction on the opportunities to take recourse, not with "match fixing" a sales process of the business. As already mentioned, the *actio Pauliana* would in any event not apply if the assets were assigned to a group company from the outset. Insofar as this matter is not covered by the *actio Pauliana*, an action on the basis of the tort of negligence is not preempted by it.[40]

---

37 *Cf.* in the context of the pre-pack R.J. de Weijs, "Wanorde? Hoe het faillissementsrecht zich tegen schuldeisers dreigt te keren," *Ondernemingsrecht* 2016/23, p. 614.

38 According to *Van Dooren q.q./ABN AMRO III (HR December 22, 2009, NJ 2010/273)*, a transaction cannot be avoided unless it is established that both the debtor and the other party have knowledge – actual or constructed – that it was a reasonable probability that insolvency proceedings would be opened against the debtor and that these proceedings would result in a deficit.

39 *Van Dooren q.q./ABN AMRO I*, HR June 16, 2000, NJ 2000/578.

40 *Cf.* HR June 16, 2000, *JOL* 2000/352, about the liability of a director of an insolvent company for his involvement in inciting employees of that company to join a competing company of that director.

Finally, liability on this basis is not dependent on the question of whether the key asset concerned once belonged to the insolvent group company. If the group was structured in this manner from the outset with the aim of locking in goodwill, the same would apply. There is an analogy in this respect with *Stichting Waaldijk/Aerts q.q.* and *Comsys/Van den End q.q.* Tortious liability is not limited to cases where existing avenues for recourse are wrongfully diminished, but also where a structure is chosen that prevents avenues of recourse from becoming available to the creditors in the first place.

However, we should bear in mind that these are exceptional cases. We know of no actual case in which liability on this basis was established or even argued, even though the separation of assets – including key assets – is commonplace. It is not only commonplace, as we explained earlier, but allowed. There is no duty on a parent company to make a group company the owner of all of the assets – or even all of the vital assets – that the latter company uses in its business.[41] Those assets may also be available to the business through a lease or any other right of use, while they are owned by another entity, be it a third party or a group company.

If the business becomes insolvent, the owner does not have a duty to keep or make the assets available to a third party that purchases the business from the insolvency practitioner.[42] This applies regardless of whether the owner is a group company or an outsider. If a local McDonald's restaurant goes bankrupt, the insolvency practitioner can try to sell the business to a third party, but McDonald's will not be obliged to entitle the third party to the use of the McDonald's logo. The third party will have to come to terms with McDonald's or to run the business under a different format. In the latter case, all McDonald's packaging, merchandise, etc. will be worthless or even constitute a liability, for instance because the third party will have to take down the McDonald's signage from above its entrance. This means that if McDonald's itself or someone licensed by McDonald's is one of the bidders, it will have an advantage over its competitors.

In the case of the local baker, the same would apply. If another company owns the building from which the bakery operates, it will not be obliged to offer a tenancy to a third party.[43] Instead, the baker will be able to start again, perhaps with the assets of the

---

41 Neither does the fact that the group operates as a single business and that all its assets are owned by group companies bring such a duty into existence. *Cf.* N. Pelletier, *La responsabilité au sein des groups de sociétés en cas de procedure collective*, diss. 2013, nr. 341-345, who remarks: "L'entreprise de groupe est à l'origine de la plupart des dettes de la filiale en difficulté mais la levee du voile social demeure exceptionelle. Le fossé se creuse et rien ne réussit à le combler." Only in extreme cases of "confusion des patrimoines et la fictivité" can this be different.

42 *See* J.M. Hummelen, *Distress dynamics*, diss. 2015, p. 161, who argues that this conforms to the law and to the theory in economics of the *creditors' bargain*. The owner has a right to refuse to cooperate outside of bankruptcy and should have this right in bankruptcy. The relative value of this right should be respected, and this value "translates in the possibility to acquire assets for a depressed value."

43 *See below* for the exception of Art. 307 of Book 7 *Burgerlijk Wetboek*.

bankrupt company. He will probably be in the position to make the best offer, because he is the only party who does not have to relocate and reassemble its assets.[44]

Of course, this limits the possibilities for a business to be transferred. If key assets are affected, transfer may not be possible at all. Value may be destroyed. That is not enough to create a duty, however.

3.3 *Insolvency Law Instruments*

This problem can be tackled by other means. Insolvency law could provide a solution. In France, for instance, Article 642-7 of the French Commercial Code (*Code de Commerce*) provides that where a business is transferred in the *liquidation judiciaire*, a court may include certain categories of essential contracts in the transfer.[45] Dutch insolvency law lacks such a provision. In certain circumstances, other law could offer a solution. Article 307 of Book 7 *Burgerlijk Wetboek*– a rule of tenancy law – opens the possibility for a tenant who intends to transfer his business to a third party to request the court to authorize him to "put the third party in his place."[46] An insolvency practitioner can also invoke this provision. That Article 40 *Faillissementswet* authorizes a landlord to terminate a tenancy if insolvency proceedings are opened against the tenant could be a problem in that case, but insolvency practitioners are sometimes able to circumvent this if the third party is able to provide assurances, not only for the future rent but also for the arrears.[47]

However, it must be stressed that the current options for retaining the use of assets owned by third parties are slim.[48] There is not much more than the above Article 307 of Book 7 *Burgerlijk Wetboek,* and even there, the cases in which it was successfully invoked in insolvency are outnumbered by those in which the attempt failed.[49]

---

44 *Cf.* the statements of Ton van Dam on the restarting of Icon Yachts from insolvency proceedings: "The insolvency practitioner had tested the deal and found it in line with market conditions. If others would have reported: fine. But the key was with the real estate and that was held by me." *See* quotenet.nl, Available at: https://www.quotenet.nl/Nieuws/Hoe-Ton-van-Dam-Icon-Yachts-failleerde-en-nog-steeds-eigenaar-is-151243 (last viewed on December 11, 2018).

45 The first three sections of this provision read: "Le tribunal détermine les contrats de crédit-bail, de location ou de fourniture de biens ou services nécessaires au maintien de l'activité au vu des observations des cocontractants du débiteur transmises au liquidateur ou à l'administrateur lorsqu'il en a été désigné.
Le jugement qui arrête le plan emporte cession de ces contrats, même lorsque la cession est précédée de la location-gérance prévue à L'Art. L. 642-13.
Ces contrats doivent être exécutés aux conditions en vigueur au jour de l'ouverture de la procédure, nonobstant toute clause contraire."

46 The first section of this provision reads: "Indien overdracht door de huurder aan een derde van het in het gehuurde door de huurder zelf of een ander uitgeoefende bedrijf gewenst wordt, kan de huurder vorderen dat hij gemachtigd wordt om die derde als huurder in zijn plaats te stellen."

47 *See*, for instance, Court of Appeal 's-Gravenhage December 23, 2008, ECLI:NL:GHSGR:2008:BG9680.

48 Even according to Art. 307 of Book 7 Dutch Civil Code.

49 *See*, for instance, District Court Overijssel December 22, 2015, ECLI:NL:RBOVE:2015:5634, Interim proceedings District Court 's-Hertogenbosch December 17, 2009, ECLI:NL:RBSHE:2009:BK8221, JOR 2010/246 and Interim proceedings District Court Rotterdam May 26, 2016, ECLI:NL:RBROT:2016:3095.

Perhaps a future *Wet continuïteit onderneming III* that aims to make the Dutch bankruptcy procedure more efficient will provide more options, but we will have to wait and see: it forms part of the *Herijking faillissementsrecht* (Recalibration of bankruptcy law) legislative action plan, but the details are not yet known.[50]

Another way of advancing the availability of key assets in business bankruptcy is demonstrated by the Belgian Article XX.87 section 2 of the Code of Economic Law (*Wetboek van Economisch Recht*).[51] It excludes parties from the bidding process that control the business or have controlled it in the six months before the opening of the insolvency proceedings and also control key assets needed for the continuation of the business, unless they make these assets available to the other bidders on the same conditions. If the business is viable *and* the controlling party has a sufficient interest in continuing the business with the risk of losing the use of the assets, the provision will have the positive effect of making key assets available, regardless of whether a group company or an outsider continues the business.

Moreover, the provision makes it impossible – or at least more difficult – to "match fix" the bidding process. If the group company is included in this process, there will be a level – or a more level – playing field because the key assets will also be available to its competitors.

However, there is a downside. If the controlling party does not want to risk the use of its assets, it is out of the race. It may, however, be the most eligible candidate – or even the only candidate – to actually purchase the business and run it efficiently. This may depress the value of the assets actually realized.[52]

We must also consider that the fact that the controlling party is out of the race does not mean that it is out of business altogether. It may acquire similar assets elsewhere, perhaps even from the bankruptcy estate if bidding for the business fails.[53] If the controlling party owns assets that are literally "key" to the bankrupt business, the bidding pro-

---

50 Reference was made to the introduction of a duty for parties to continue at least some executory contracts (Letter of the Minister of Security and Justice to the President of the House of Representatives of November 26, 2012, Parliamentary Documents II). 2012/2013, 29911, 74).

51 This section states: "Ingeval een offerte uitgaat van personen die controle op de onderneming uitoefenen of hebben uitgeoefend gedurende zes maanden voorafgaand aan de opening van de procedure, en die rechtstreeks of onrechtstreeks de controle hebben over rechten die noodzakelijk zijn voor de voortzetting van haar activiteiten, kan die offerte slechts in aanmerking worden genomen op voorwaarde dat die rechten onder dezelfde voorwaarden toegankelijk zijn voor de andere bieders."

52 The question is similar to the exclusion from the bidding process of parties that are affiliated to the debtor, as in France. *See* Art. 642-3 of the French Commercial Code, cited in footnote 35.

53 Art. XX.87 section 2 does not prevent this. *Cf.* the above Art. 642-3 French Commercial Code, which adds (in section 1, second sentence) to the exclusion of affiliated parties from the bidding process a prohibition on acquiring assets that are comprised in the transfer of the business: "De même, il est fait interdiction à ces personnes d'acquérir, dans les cinq années suivant la cession, tout ou partie des biens compris dans cette cession, directement ou indirectement, ainsi que d'acquérir des parts ou titres de capital de toute société ayant dans son patrimoine, directement ou indirectement, tout ou partie de ces biens, ainsi que des valeurs mobilières donnant accès, dans le même délai, au capital de cette société."

cess will fail because no other party will be able to continue the bankrupt company's business and compete with the controlling party.

Whether the positive effects of such a provision outweigh its negative effects remains to be seen.

4 Concluding Remarks

Currently, Dutch law provides considerable room for the parties to divide assets between different legal entities. The basis for this is the principle of party autonomy against a backdrop of freedom of enterprise. However, this is not to say that there are no limits to strategically partitioning assets. The Dutch Supreme Court has set boundaries to the courses of conduct that are particularly detrimental to creditors, especially in the field of tortious liability. Where group companies are divided into loss-making and profitable parts – which is fairly common in practice – this can create disproportionate risks for the loss-making company's creditors. Even though such corporate structures are not unlawful in themselves, establishing a structure that is inherently risky for creditors can allow liability to be constructed toward a company's joint creditors.

In particular, if intragroup dealings are not fair from a commercial perspective, the parent company runs the risk of being held liable for losses to creditors. In addition, where assets are assigned to another person or legal entity with the predominant objective of preventing creditors from taking recourse against these assets, this is likely to result in liability for the loss that the creditors suffer. This case law reveals that actions obstructing avenues for recourse do not always need to have occurred near the moment of insolvency for liability to be found. The basis for liability lies in the creation of an asset structure that implies disproportionate risks for creditors.

The state of the law is less developed regarding the consequences of asset partitioning on maintaining value in insolvency. As a starting point, it has been argued in this report that following from the core principles of private law, such as party autonomy, parties are allowed to manage their affairs as they wish. If they wish to operate an enterprise from a group structure and divide its assets between companies for the purpose of spreading business risks, this is not at odds with any principle or rule of law. While there is no duty to divide the assets in a group in such a way as to maximize the value of particular companies, limits to this freedom can emerge in the light of creditors' interests.

We argued that if the assets are distributed among a group's companies with a view to ensuring that the surplus value – the goodwill – of one will not be available to its creditors but can be realized only by an affiliated company, this may constitute negligence toward the general body of creditors. The "locking in" of a business should not be a legally appropriate aim to pursue. At present, Dutch law contains no duties for parent companies to maximize the value of an insolvent business by making key or other assets available to third parties.

Selective Perforation by Means of Guarantees: Dutch Law

Aart Jonkers[*]

"The 800-pound gorilla in the corner that goes unnoticed"[1]

1 Introduction

By means of limited liability and separate legal personality, groups can incorporate in ways where liabilities and assets are allocated to different legal entities. After division into subsidiaries, the first step is often to selectively perforate the newly created limited liability structure in favor of financial creditors.[2] The question could be asked whether, in such a selectively pierced group structure, the separateness of the legal entities the group consists of can still be taken seriously. This question and the approach of Dutch law to this question are briefly discussed in Section 2. A bankruptcy administrator could, in theory, attack the guarantee itself with transaction avoidance law, but Dutch law is underdeveloped on this point, as discussed in Section 3.

Counterintuitively, in practice the legal rules applicable to group guarantees seem very friendly to financial creditors. Dutch law, for example, often provides that guaranteed creditors can claim up to the full amount in the different insolvency proceedings when various group companies are declared insolvent. This issue is discussed in Section 4.

Moreover, such guarantees give an incentive to the group companies to make selective payments to the guaranteed creditor, as such payments indirectly benefit the possibly surviving group companies. In case of distress of certain group companies, this incentive becomes stronger. In that sense, intergroup guarantees can be seen as promises to the lender to make preferential payments, especially on the eve of bankruptcy. This dynamic has been almost completely overlooked in Dutch law and literature. These points are discussed in Section 5.

---

* Aart Jonkers is a teacher and researcher at the Centre for the Study of European Contract Law, University of Amsterdam.

1 Derived from a quote by Widen: " (...) if secured lending presents fairness problems, the unsecured syndicated guarantee may be the 800-pound gorilla in the corner that goes unnoticed."; W. Widen, "Corporate Form and Substantive Consolidation," *The George Washington Law Review*, Vol. 75, No. 2, 2007, p. 309.

2 R. Squire, "Strategic Liability in the Corporate Group," *The University of Chicago Law Review*, Vol. 78, 2011, p. 606.

2 DUTCH LAW ON VEIL PIERCING IN RELATION TO SELECTIVELY PIERCED GROUP STRUCTURES

The international literature has recognized that the arguments justifying limited liability of a legal entity are much less strong within a corporate group[3] and again less strong when those group entities have selectively pierced their limited liability shield by guarantees to major creditors.[4] How does Dutch law deal with these insights? One would expect the law to sooner allow for veil piercing when group entities have pierced the group structure with guarantees, but there is little evidence that this is the case under Dutch law.

Both in public and private companies, shareholders of the company are not personally liable for the (unpaid) debts of the corporation (Art. 2:64 paragraph 1 BW and 2:175 paragraph 1 BW, respectively). However, in case of abuse of legal personality, a court could equate the legal person with its shareholder(s), thus burdening the shareholder with all the debts of the legal person, effectively canceling legal personality and thus limited liability. Dutch courts hardly ever do so.[5] Necessary conditions for such equation probably include a clear case of abuse of legal personality with the purpose of avoiding opportunities for recovery by creditors.[6] Next to direct veil piercing, creditors and/or the bankruptcy administrator could pursue shareholders on the basis of tort (Art. 6:162 BW), often referred to as indirect veil piercing. If such a claim succeeds, the boundaries between the shareholder and the company it holds shares in are not completely disregarded, but the shareholder is de facto held liable for some specific debt(s) of the company. The question is whether shareholders can generally be more easily held liable because they have already voluntarily pierced the veil by giving one creditor a guarantee.

Relevant in this context is that, next to liability for distributions, the Dutch Supreme Court has also set out the conditions for holding shareholders responsible for (certain) debts of the subsidiary on the basis of Article 6:162 BW (tort law) in situations of un-

3 A.A. Berle, "The Theory of Enterprise Entity," *Columbia Law Review,* Vol. 47, No. 6, 1947, pp. 343-358; F.H. Easterbrook & D.R. Fischel, "Limited Liability and the Corporation," *The University of Chicago Law Review,* Vol. 52, No. 1, 1985, pp. 110-111; H. Hansmann & R. Squire, "External and Internal Asset Partitioning: Corporations and Their Subsidiaries," *in* J.N. Gordon & W.G. Ringe, *The Oxford Handbook of Corporate Law and Governance,* Oxford University Press, 2016, para. 3; P.I. Blumberg, "Limited Liability and Corporate Groups," *The Journal of Corporation Law,* 1986, pp. 623-626; T.K. Cheng, "An Economic Analysis of Limited Shareholder Liability in Contractual Claims," *Berkeley Business Law Journal,* Vol. 11, No. 1, 2014, pp. 112-181; G.C. Rapp, "Preserving LLC Veil Piercing: A Response to Bainbridge," *The Journal of Corporation Law,* 2006, p. 1094; K. Vanderkerckhove, *Piercing the Corporate Veil,* Alphen aan den Rijn, Kluwer Law International, 2007, p. 9.

4 Hansmann & Squire, 2016, para. 3.

5 Asser/Maeijer, Van Solinge & Nieuwe Weme 2-II*, *De naamloze en besloten vennootschap,* Deventer, Kluwer, 2009, nr. 836.

6 *See* J. Barneveld, *Financiering en Vermogensonttrekking door Aandeelhouders,* Deventer, Kluwer, 2014, pp. 470-471; The Dutch Supreme Court case Krijger/Citco (June 9, 1995, *NJ* 1996, 213) is also often mentioned in this context, although the case is strictly not about veil piercing, *see also* L. Groenewoud, "Vereenzelviging als grond tot doorbraak van aansprakelijkheid," *Vennootschap & Onderneming,* No. 1, 2003, pp. 4-5.

justifiably continuing the company.[7] In short, a parent company (or shareholder) can be held liable if there are close ties between shareholder and company with the accompanying power of intervention of the shareholder,[8] which leads to the conclusion that the parent has some duty of care toward creditors of the subsidiary, while this duty has been breached at a certain point by not acting on a moment that the subsidiary is in a deplorable financial state and the shareholder knows, or should have known, that new creditors would be prejudiced.[9] This category of shareholder liability is often referred to as liability for creating an appearance of creditworthiness. The parent company can be held liable for the claims of creditors on their subsidiary if these claims came into existence after the moment that the parent should have acted. Whereas the earlier case law of the Dutch Supreme Court led many to believe that liability could occur only if this appearance of creditworthiness was created actively,[10] for example by the shareholder communicating to creditors that he would continue to financially support their debtor,[11] later case law seems to allow for the possibility of claiming on the parent even if the parent did not actively create the appearance.[12]

It is important to note that the mere fact that the parent has financed the subsidiary, directly with loans or indirectly with guarantees, and stops this financing at some point, can in itself probably not lead to the conclusion that the parent can be held liable for creating an appearance of creditworthiness.[13] A shareholder that still invests in the company prior to insolvency, and thus takes risk himself, is often actually less likely to be held liable for creating an appearance of creditworthiness.[14] In that sense, the fact that a shareholder guarantees or has guaranteed certain debts of the company could, counterintuitively, make it more likely that the shareholder escapes liability toward other creditors.

There are also some cases in which liability of shareholders was not based on not acting by the shareholders at a moment at which bankruptcy of the debtor was foreseeable, but as such on the dubious corporate structure of which the bankrupt debtor was

---

7 Most notable are: Dutch Supreme Court September 25, 1981, *NJ 1982, 443* (Osby); Dutch Supreme Court September 12, 2008, *JOR* 2008/297 (Van Dusseldorp/Coutts Holding); Dutch Supreme Court February 19, 1988, *NJ* 1988, 487 (Albada Jelgersma); Dutch Supreme Court November 18, 1994, *NJ* 1995, 170 (NBM/Securicor); Dutch Supreme Court December 21, 2001, *JOR* 2002/38 (Sobi/Hurks).

8 *See* particularly Dutch Supreme Court December 21, 2001, *JOR* 2002/38 (Sobi/Hurks) and the case note by Bartman; *see also* Asser/Maeijer, Van Solinge & Nieuwe Weme 2-II*, 2009, nr. 842.

9 Dutch Supreme Court December 21, 2001, *JOR* 2002/38 (Sobi/Hurks).

10 *See* case note Bartman to Dutch Supreme Court December 21, 2001, *JOR* 2002/38 (Sobi/Hurks).

11 *See* for such a case Dutch Supreme Court February 19, 1988, *NJ* 1988, 487 (Albada Jelgersma).

12 Dutch Supreme Court December 21, 2001, *JOR* 2002/38 (Sobi/Hurks); *see also* Asser/Maeijer, Van Solinge & Nieuwe Weme 2-II*, 2009, nr. 842.

13 *See* the Court of Appeal case that led to Dutch Supreme Court September 12, 2008, *JOR* 2008/297 (Van Dusseldorp q.q./Coutts Holding).

14 *See* para. 4.20 of the Advocate General's opinion to Dutch Supreme Court September 12, 2008, *JOR* 2008/297 (Van Dusseldorp q.q./Coutts Holding).

part. Such cases are, however, rare. The leading case before the Dutch Supreme Court is Comsys.[15] This case has been extensively discussed in the first part of this report on Dutch law, by Verstijlen & Karapatian. The relevance of this type of liability to selectively pierced group structures is that operating a group such as the one in the *Comsys* case is often essentially made possible by piercing guarantees. Strangely enough, this is not as such discussed in the *Comsys* case itself, although piercing guarantees were very likely in place. The Court of Appeal does mention that there was one credit contract between the whole Comsys group and Rabobank and that Comsys Services had pledged all its assets to Rabobank. These circumstances are almost unthinkable without each group member guaranteeing the whole debt. Because of these guarantees, Rabobank did not have to care much about the internal group structure. The parent profits from the structure, the major lender that makes the structure possible by financing does not care about the structure because all group companies have issued guarantees to the bank, and the creditors that probably had no knowledge of the structure are prejudiced. The guarantees are a crucial part of making the structure practically possible.

In short, Dutch law does not clearly consider the guarantee by a shareholder a relevant factor in shareholder liability cases. In that sense, Dutch law pays little attention to the opaque priority structure that the guarantee and incorporation together can create.

3 Avoiding the Guarantee Itself

An alternative legal response to tearing down the limited liability walls in order to address the inefficiencies of certain perforated limited liability structures is to reinstate the walls by giving certain actors such as other creditors or the bankruptcy administrator the power to annul the guarantee. Under Dutch law, an avoidance action (*actio pauliana*) seems most suitable to this end, though it will often be difficult to apply. Other instruments to avoid (the effects of) a piercing guarantee that may come to mind are an action based on the doctrine of *ultra vires* (*doeloverschrijding*) and an action based on conflict of interest of the directors involved. Both these actions are, however, excessively hard to apply to the situation discussed. These actions thus need little further discussion.

Under Dutch law, the bankruptcy administrator can avoid certain acts that the debtor performed before bankruptcy, the so-called actio pauliana. Within transaction avoidance law, the Dutch doctrine distinguishes between legal acts that the debtor was obliged to perform (Art. 42 Fw) and acts that were not required by a preexisting legal duty (Art. 47 Fw). Acts that were required by a preexisting legal duty are generally (much) more difficult to avoid for a bankruptcy administrator. If a group entity guarantees group debt toward a lender, this may be on request of the parent or holding company. Such an

15 Dutch Supreme Court September 11, 2009, NJ 2009/565 (Comsys/Van den End q.q.) with case note by H.J. Snijders and P. van Schilfgaarde.

instruction by the parent does, however, not make issuing the guarantee "obliged" in the sense of Article 47 Fw. Only legal obligations toward the counterparty of the contested act qualify as obligations in the sense of Article 47 Fw.[16] Unless the debtor committed himself toward the creditor to issue the guarantee prior to guaranteeing, the bankruptcy administrator can rely on Article 42 Fw in trying to avoid the act.

For the application of Article 42 Fw, the bankruptcy administrator should, next to showing that there was no legal duty to perform the act, show the act brought prejudice to the creditors and that both the debtor and the counterparty had knowledge of such prejudice (Art. 42 Fw). Knowledge of prejudice on the part of the counterparty does not have to be shown by the bankruptcy administrator in the case that the act was for no consideration, and if such act for no consideration was performed within less than one year prior to insolvency, knowledge of prejudice is presumed to exist on the part of the debtor (Art. 45 Fw). These exceptions may apply to issuing guarantees in the context of group finance if it can be shown that the debtor in no way profited from issuing the guarantee. In the case *X q.q./Van Doorn Beheer*, the Court of Appeal found that a guarantee of an ex-subsidiary, that guaranteed the debt of the buyer of the shares of that subsidiary toward the ex-parent company, was an act without consideration.[17] More generally, however, the courts are likely to assume that indirect benefits from the guarantee will qualify as consideration.[18] Most guarantees for group debt, or guarantees by natural persons for debts of a limited liability corporation in which they hold shares, will thus probably qualify as acts for consideration.

Secondly, prejudice to creditors needs to be shown. The Dutch Supreme Court has a rather broad understanding of prejudice, which makes proving prejudice generally no issue for the bankruptcy administrator.[19] Showing (somewhat objectified) *knowledge* of prejudice is generally, however, hard, especially on the side of the counterparty. The yardstick that the Supreme Court has formulated is that such knowledge exists on the side of the counterparty if it can be shown that bankruptcy and a deficit in such bankruptcy, which implies prejudice to creditors, could have been forecast with reasonable probability.[20] This is generally hard to show.

The bankruptcy administrator is, however, helped with the evidentiary presumptions of knowledge of prejudice (on both the side of the creditor and that of the debtor) of

16 P. van Schilfgaarde, "Aantasting van concernfinanciering door de actio pauliana en de actie uit onrechtmatige daad," *in* Honee, Lievens & Van der Grinten, *Financële kruisverbanden en andere aspecten van concernfinanciering*, Deventer, Kluwer, 1987, p. 86; compare also District Court of The Hague (president) June 23, 1992, KG 1992/343. *See* on that case also M.Ph van Sint Truiden, "Intra-groep-garanties en de (actio) pauliana," *Bedrijfsjuridische Berichten*, No. 25, 1992, pp. 223-225.

17 Arnhem-Leeuwarden Court of Appeal, February 12, 2013, ECLI:NL:GHARL:2013:822, *JOR* 2013/78.

18 Dutch Supreme Court July 13, 2012, JOR 2012/306 (Janssen q.q./JVS).

19 Dutch Supreme Court October 19, 2001, ECLI:NL:HR:2001:ZC3654, NJ 2001, 654 (Diepstraten/Gilhuis q.q.); Dutch Supreme Court July 8, 2005, NJ 2005, 457, JOR 2005/230 (Van Dooren q.q./ABN AMRO II).

20 Dutch Supreme Court December 22, 2009, ECLI:NL:HR:2009:BI8493, *NJ* 2010, 273 (Van Dooren q.q. / ABN AMRO III).

Article 43 Fw, which presumptions may apply to the case of guarantees in the context of group finance and guarantees by business owners. The first requirement for the presumption to apply is that the guarantee was issued within one year prior to insolvency. For older guarantees, the bankruptcy administrator will always have to show that bankruptcy and a deficit in such bankruptcy could have been forecast with reasonable probability by both parties to the transaction.

If the guarantee was issued in the year prior to bankruptcy, the presumption applies only if one of the following alternative conditions is also met: (1) the transaction was at an undervalue; (2) the transaction was a payment on or security for old debt that was not yet due; (3) the counterparty was a related party, as defined in Article 43 paragraph 1 (3)(4) (5) and paragraphs 2-6. The background of these requirements is that Article 43 Fw describes particularly suspect categories of transactions that should more easily be up for avoidance.

The first alternative condition, transactions at undervalue, is complicated to apply to guarantees. As discussed earlier, even guarantees for which no direct premium is paid will usually be viewed as "for consideration." That does not mean that the up- and downside to the guarantor were sufficiently balanced. If, in the group context, the debtor that issued the guarantee hardly used the credit facility, this may lead to the conclusion that, while there may have been consideration, the transaction was performed at an undervalue.[21] If the transaction was at an undervalue because the profit the debtor had from the transaction was disproportional to the liability incurred, the creditor could possibly argue that he did not have to have insight into the internal relations of his debtors.[22] Whether this suffices is unsure and probably dependent on the circumstances. As Van Schilfgaarde argues, this defense becomes difficult to maintain if the liability of the debtor under the guarantee exceeds the size of the patrimony of the debtor.[23] The focus in applying this requirement is on what the upside was for the guarantor and what liability was incurred, and to what extent these are in balance. As shown by Squire, this focus does not track the efficiency analysis of such guarantees.[24] The focus should be on the question of the extent to which the fate of the guarantor and that of the debtor were correlated. The more they were correlated, the more likely that the guarantee defrauded other creditors.

The presumption also applies if the guarantee was assumed for an older debt that was not yet due (Art. 43 paragraph 1 sub 2).[25] Guarantees are probably often granted for such old debts that are not yet due, but, by definition, not debts of the debtor himself but debts of others. The requirements thus do not apply directly. One could convincingly argue for analogous application, but there is no leading case law on this point.

---

21 *See also* Van Schilfgaarde, 1987, pp. 86-87.
22 Van Schilfgaarde, 1987, p. 87.
23 Van Schilfgaarde, 1987, p. 87.
24 Squire, 2011.
25 If the guarantee was given for a new debt, this presumption does not apply; *see* Dutch Supreme Court November 29, 2013, *NJ* 2014/9 (Roeffen q.q./Jaya).

The same applies to the alternative condition of related party transactions in Article 43 paragraph 1 (3)(4)(5) and paragraphs 2-6. These apply in the case that the counterparty is such a related party of the debtor. Where the debtor guarantees group debt or debts of a legal person he holds shares in, the counterparty is often not a related party, whereas the principal debtor obviously is. Again, the presumption of Article 43 thus does not apply directly to acts in the year before bankruptcy. Analog application is somewhat harder to argue here, as the act is avoided by a successful action that comes directly to the detriment of the unrelated creditor.

In short, reinstating the walls by avoiding guarantees is difficult under Dutch law. Guarantees that have been granted longer than a year before bankruptcy are very hard to avoid, as knowledge of prejudice to creditors on both sides (interpreted as reasonably have been able to foresee bankruptcy) will have to be shown. In the year before bankruptcy, an evidentiary presumption as to this requirement may apply, but this is not obvious and is likely to be controversial. All this is only the case if the guarantee was voluntarily granted. If there was a legal obligation for the debtor to issue the guarantee, for example on the basis of earlier contracts, the guarantee is even harder to avoid.

4 DUTCH LAW ON DOUBLE PROOF[26]

Double proof occurs when a creditor is able to make more than one claim in relation to a single debt. This mechanism can, depending on the legal rules, occur in different degrees of strength. The following example will explain this:

Consider a bank that has an unsecured claim of 90. There are 10 other unsecured creditors, each with a claim of 10. The debtor has assets worth 100. In the case of distribution in insolvency, each would receive 26% (see figure 1).

26 This section is partly based on my article in a Dutch law journal: A.L. Jonkers, “Persoonlijke zekerheden bij concernfinanciering: ongerechtvaardigde vermenigvuldiging van vorderingen,” *Maandblad voor Vermogensrecht*, No. 5, 2018, pp. 164-171.

Figure 1 Simple case without guarantees

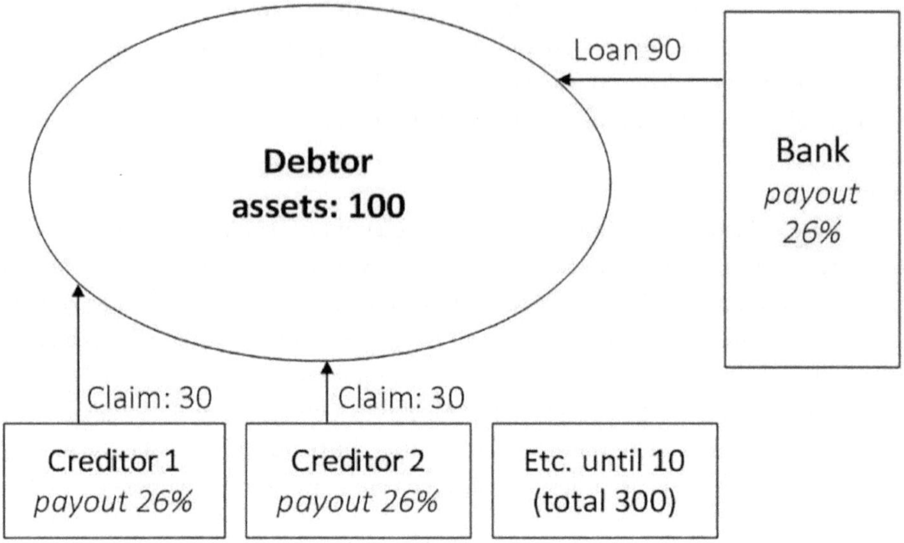

As a variation, consider that the debtor is not one single entity but is subdivided into a holding company and 9 subsidiary entities, each with limited liability. Everything else stays the same, though the bank has provided the loan to the holding company with guarantees of all subsidiaries for the full sum, as is common in group finance. All other creditors only have a claim in relation to one single debtor, and each on a different subsidiary. If, in a bankruptcy of all the group entities, the bank were allowed to submit its claim of 90 in each bankruptcy proceeding, a strong form of double (or actually 10-fold) proof would occur. The bank is able to make ten claims of 90, thus total 900, while it has only made a loan of 90. The payout of the bank rises to 83%, while the other creditors are left with 8.3% each (see figure 2).[27] Because of this squeeze-down effect on unsecured creditors of double proof through guarantees, W. Widen has, rightly, referred to inter-company guarantees as "the 800-pound gorilla in the room that goes unnoticed."[28]

Most legal systems do not allow such double proof in the context of real security rights. If double proof is not allowed, the creditor would get only a percentage of the proceeds of the unencumbered assets based on the *unsecured* part of his claim.

---

27 *See* further, also for other numerical examples, Widen, 2007, p. 307 ff; this example is not used to suggest that this would be the main reason for banks and companies to structure the company and the loan in this way. There are many reasons why subdividing into subsidiaries may be functional; *see also* E.B. Rock, "Adapting to the new shareholder-centric reality," *University of Pennsylvania Law Review*, 2013, pp. 1968-1969.

28 Widen, 2007, p. 309.

Figure 2 Strong-form double proof

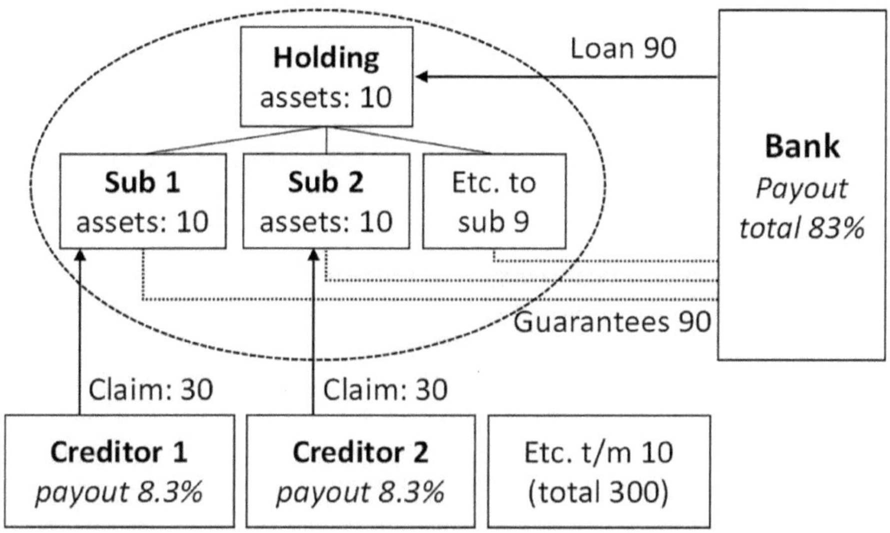

From the perspective of the bankruptcy proceeding of an individual group entity of a bankrupt group, double proof can also lead to odd results. Assume an individual group company that is relatively small, for example with a balance sheet total of 300.000, whereas the group has a balance sheet total of 50 million. The group, as a whole, may have used a credit line of 20 million, guaranteed by all individual group companies. The total of creditors (other than the bank) of the individual group company could be 400.000, whereas there could, after liquidation, only be 200.000 in assets to distribute, amounting to a payout of 50%. However, the bank also submits its claim of 20 million, even though this individual group company obviously did not use the full credit facility of 20 million. Admission of this claim would reduce the payout to creditors to roughly (200.000 divided by 20.4 million =) 1%. The 200.000 thus almost entirely goes to the guaranteed bank, the other creditors are left with barely nothing, while they (probably) actually extended credit to this entity, whereas the bank merely extended credit to the group as a whole.

Cases become extreme when real security rights are taken into the equation. What if the credit line in the preceding example was almost fully secured, for example with 19 million worth of real security rights. Allowing the creditor to still submit a claim of 20 million in the bankruptcy cases of subsidiaries that have not granted real security rights would look strange. Things get even stranger when the possibility of credit bidding is also taken into the equation. What if the secured and guaranteed creditor uses the guarantee claim to place a credit bid on the assets on which he has security rights? He could make a bid up to the face amount of the claim, without having to pay anything (as he holds the security right), thus keeping a strong grip on the assets. Still, a rule that allows double proof would allow him to still claim the same amount in the bankruptcy cases of other subsidiaries (or to make more credit bids) that have guaranteed the debt.

The preceding example (figure 2) may need some explanation in regard to the nature and appearance of double proof. If the bank in the example extended a total of 90 credit to 10 group companies, and thus has a claim of 90 on each, the strongest version of double proofing would mean that, in the case of a group insolvency, the bank can claim 90 in each insolvency, disregarding any payments the bank receives on the debt after the date of bankruptcy filing. I call this *strong-form double proof*.

Two variations can be conceptualized. In the first, the bank would only be allowed to submit his deficiency claim in each insolvency, which would mean 90 in the first and, if the payout in the first is 8.3% (= 7.5) (as in the preceding example), 90 minus 7.5 = 82.5 in the second, etc. This could be referred to as *deficiency double proof*. Deficiency double proof essentially still allows for double proofing, but just for smaller amounts. If the guaranteed creditor can share pro rata in the distribution in the first bankruptcy based on a claim of 90, and after receiving 7.5 can share pro rata in the second bankruptcy based on a claim of 82.5, double proofing still occurs but just for smaller amounts. The guaranteed creditor now gets a combined return of roughly 72%,[29] compared with (on average) 12%[30] for the other creditors. Although he only extended 90 of credit, he is able to, in the ten bankruptcy cases combined, assert a total claim of 593[31] (down from 900 in the case of strong-form double proof), squeezing down ordinary creditors that are only able to assert the amount of their claim once and in one bankruptcy proceeding. In short, if the guaranteed creditor is only allowed to assert deficiency claims against each codebtor, double proof still occurs, but just in a weaker form.

Dutch law allows *strong-form double proof*; the 800-pound gorilla indeed goes unnoticed. Article 136 Fw regulates some specific questions that could arise in the context of an insolvent principal debtor who is the beneficiary of a guarantee relationship. This provision, that generally applies to debtors that are severally liable, states in paragraph 1 that the creditor can submit the full amount of his claim, measured on the day of the declaration of bankruptcy, in the insolvency proceedings of his debtor, and if there are more bankrupt severally liable debtors, in each insolvency proceeding. In essence, this article stipulates that *strong-form double proof* is allowed without restrictions. If, for ex-

29 The payment per bankruptcy case (in the example of figure 2, but with a rule of deficiency double proof) is then: ((10/120) × 90 = 7.5) + ((10/112.50) × 82.5 = 7.3) + ((10/105.2) × 75.2 = 7.15) + ((10/98.05) × 68.05 = 6.94) + ((10/91.11) × 61.11 = 6.71) + ((10/84.4) × 54.4 = 6.45) + ((10/77.95) × 47.95 = 6.15) + ((10/71.8) × 41.8 = 5.82) + ((10/68.98) × 38.98 = 5.65) + ((10/63.33) × 33.33 = 5.26) = total 64.93 payment on a claim of 90, which amounts to a 72% pay-out.

30 The total of assets in all bankruptcies combined was 100. 100 minus 64.93 (*see supra* footnote 29)= 35.7, which is the total distribution to the other creditor, who together have a total claim of 300. 35.7/300 × 100% = 12%.

31 *See* footnote above, 90 + 82.5 + 75.2 + 68.05 + 61.11 + 54.4 + 47.95 + 41.8 + 38.98 + 33.33 = 593.33.

ample, five severally liable debtors are declared bankrupt on the same day and the creditor has a claim of 100 on them, the creditor can submit 100 in each insolvency proceeding. If he gets paid 20 in one bankruptcy proceeding on, say, day 10, he can, also after day 10, still pursue a claim of 100 in the proceedings of the other four. Article 136 paragraph 1 Fw is a strange exception to the rule of Article 6:7 paragraph 2 BW, which stipulates that performance by one severally liable debtor discharges the other debtors as well.

Strong-form double proof was widely criticized in Dutch legal literature in the late 19th century[32] and is (not surprisingly) still criticized,[33] but changes have never been considered by the legislature or courts, which is striking given the fact that double proof is not allowed with real security rights. If the creditor has real security rights, he can submit only the unsecured part of the claim in the insolvency of the debtor (Art. 59 Fw), not the full claim. No attention whatsoever has been given to the problem of *deficiency double proof*. Even the critics of *strong-form double proof* did not discuss that the same problem essentially remains in a slightly weaker form when only deficiency claims on guaranteed debt can be submitted.

Double proof becomes especially problematic in relation to credit bids. The term credit bidding is used to describe a practice in which a creditor with security rights over certain property bids on the property in an execution sale. Such a bid is done in paper money, as the receiving party is the creditor himself, at least in as far as the creditor has an outstanding claim. The creditor can thus make a bid up to the amount of his outstanding claim without having to provide actual money. As discussed earlier, creditors, in the context of group finance, can have artificially high claims on all group entities because of guarantees. Without any considerable brakes on either double proof or credit bids, the creditor could use these artificially high amounts to make artificially high credit bids on all the property over which he also holds real security rights, thus keeping strong control over the debtor's property, without such credit bids affecting his claims over other group companies (although one could argue that making such bids again and again allows the creditor to, on paper, receive more than 100%, which should not be allowed). Dutch law does not provide any substantial brakes on credit bidding.[34]

---

32 *See* for an overview W.H. van Boom, *Hoofdelijke Verbintenissen*, Deventer, W.E.J. Tjeenk Willink, 1999, pp. 84-88.

33 Van Boom, 1999, pp. 87, 237-238; C.J.M. Klaassen, "10 Jaar Hoofdelijkheid en Borgtocht naar 'NBW'," *in* Kortmann, Janssen, Solinge & Faber, *Onderneming en 10 Jaar Nieuw Burgerlijk Recht*, Deventer, Kluwer, 2002, p. 696; *See*, however, G.J.L. Bergervoet, *Borgtocht*, Deventer, Kluwer, 2014, who approves of the extra bonus for the creditor, arguing this accommodates expedient settlement of the insolvency proceedings.

34 *See also* R.J. de Weijs & G.A.C. Orban, "Loan-to-Own meets Credit Bid: Credit Bidding naar Amerikaans en Nederlands recht," *Tijdschrift voor Insolventierecht*, No. 3, 2016, pp. 111-119.

5 SELECTIVE PAYMENTS TO GUARANTEED CREDITORS

Not unrelated, but clearly distinguishable from the treatment of pierced group structures and double proof is the behavior that the guarantee incentivizes *after* concluding the guarantee. Guarantees are likely to influence the borrower to favor the guaranteed lender above others by making payments or in another way transferring value to the guaranteed lender before insolvency. In other words, the guarantee creates incentives to act opportunistically in favor of the guaranteed lender to the detriment of other creditors. The reason why is simple. The incentives of the guarantor are clearly influenced by the guarantee relationship: the guarantor will have a high preference for preventing default of the debtor in relation to the guaranteed creditor and will care less about default of the debtor toward other creditors. There will, in other words, be an incentive for selective payment of the guaranteed creditor. Illustrative is the explanation of a bank manager interviewed by Mann on the question of why he requests guarantees from managers/shareholders of borrowers:

> When we get into trouble, where the company runs into difficulty, we find that the borrower's owners are much more willing to help us when they're personally liable.[35]

Simply put, the guarantee relationship by an insider leads to preferential treatment of the guaranteed creditor, from which the noninsider creditor also profits. The same, of course, applies to guarantees of group companies for other group companies. The group companies will have a high preference for paying off guaranteed debt first, as such payments indirectly lower the exposure of other group companies toward the guaranteed creditor. In the case of distress, this incentive becomes stronger. A guarantee could thus be seen as a promise to make preferential payments on the eve of bankruptcy.

This section will discuss how Dutch law deals with such preferential payments. Various mechanisms under Dutch law that may be relevant in this context are discussed below: first and foremost, preference law, but also shareholder liability, director liability, and lender liability. This section concludes that Dutch law hardly regulates the dynamics, thus leaving too much room for opportunistic preferential payments.

35 R.J. Mann, "The Role of Secured Credit in Small-Business Lending," *The Georgetown Law Journal*, Vol. 86, No. 1, 1998, p. 24, quoting from an interview with Carmen Mastroianni, Senior Vice-President, Chase Manhattan Corp.

5.1 *Preference Law*

Transaction avoidance law may deter the leverage that a lender can obtain through a guarantee, thus deterring the incentive for insider dealing. If a principal debtor is in financial trouble, he or persons involved in the principal debtor (if the principal debtor is a company) may have incentive to give preference to a guaranteed lender above other creditors. This could happen in the context of group finance, in which a parent company may prefer its subsidiary to pay creditors guaranteed by the parent before other creditors when the subsidiary is approaching bankruptcy or, in the case of small-business finance, in which a shareholder or manager that guaranteed business debt may have the same inclination. The motivation to pay off guaranteed debt first is driven by the fact that the guarantor indirectly profits from such payments, because his exposure under the guarantee is reduced by the same amount. In Dutch law, there is no specific regulation dealing with the problem of the indirect profit that the guarantor receives by limiting his exposure through influence on the principal debtor.[36] Dutch transaction avoidance law has great difficulty dealing with such indirect preferences.

Dutch transaction avoidance law does not clearly distinguish between preferences given to a creditor and other actions of the debtor that have diminished the insolvent estate. Instead, a distinction is made between legal acts (*rechtshandelingen*)[37] that were voluntary in the sense that there was no legal obligation to perform the act (Art. 42 Fw) and legal acts that were obligatory (Art. 47 Fw). Legal acts that were obligatory, such as due payments, are generally near impossible to avoid, whereas legal acts that were voluntary can more easily be avoided. The test for the latter is whether the creditors have been prejudiced and whether both debtor and counterparty had knowledge of such prejudice to creditors (Art. 42 Fw). The Dutch Supreme Court has a very broad understanding of prejudice to creditors, so this will often be easy to show.[38] Knowledge of prejudice to creditors is explained as having been able to foresee bankruptcy of the debtor and a shortfall in such a bankruptcy with reasonable probability.

If a payment on a guaranteed debt was voluntary, avoidance of the payment is, in principle, rather simple, though not because of the existence of the guarantee, but simply because Article 43 paragraph 1 sub 2 Fw presumes that payments within one year prior to insolvency on debts that are not due were accompanied by knowledge of prejudice to creditors on both the side of the principal debtor and that of the counterparty (the guar-

36 *See also* R.J. De Weijs, "Financieren met Garanties door Aandeelhouders: Vergeten Problematiek," *FIP: Tijdschrift Financiering, Zekerheden en Insolventierechtpraktijk*, No. 6, 2010, p. 162.

37 Only legal acts can be avoided with transaction avoidance law. Other actions of the debtor that have been detrimental to the creditor cannot be attacked by transaction avoidance law. In order to undo the consequences of such nonlegal acts, the bankruptcy administrator would often have to rely on unjustified enrichment (Art. 6:212 BW) or tort (Art. 6:162 BW).

38 Dutch Supreme Court October 19, 2001, ECLI:NL:HR:2001:ZC3654, NJ 2001, 654 (Diepstraten/Gilhuis q.q.); Dutch Supreme Court July 8, 2005, NJ 2005, 457, JOR 2005/230 (Van Dooren q.q./ABN AMRO II).

anteed creditor). Rebuttal of the presumption will be difficult outside exceptional circumstances, as payment of undue debts at a moment that there are also (many) due debts to pay, will always be suspect. However, avoidance on the basis of Article 42 (in conjunction with Art. 43) Fw only allows payment to be retrieved from the direct counterparty of that payment, not from the person that indirectly profited from such payment (here the guarantor). The fact that the insider guarantor profits indirectly, and thus has engaged in insider dealing, is usually not considered directly relevant in this context.

The question whether there was prejudice to creditors in the context of a guarantee relationship has come before the Dutch Supreme Court in a somewhat complicated case. The parent company had guaranteed the debt of a subsidiary toward the bank. The parent company had also bought caravans from the subsidiary and paid the subsidiary for the caravans on the bank account of the subsidiary. Because there was an overdraft on the bank account, the payment essentially satisfied part of the claim of the bank and thus limited the exposure of the parent company toward the bank under the guarantee. The Court of Appeal had held that the sale of and payment for the caravans could not have prejudiced the other creditors, because a fair price was paid for the caravans. The Supreme Court, however, held that even though the price was fair, there was prejudice to the other creditors because the proceeds of the transaction went directly to the bank (and indirectly benefited the parent company), while the other creditors were left empty-handed (regarding these proceeds).[39] It is questionable how important the indirect benefit to the parent was for the Supreme Court to come to this conclusion. Also absent the guarantee, the Supreme Court would possibly find that there was prejudice to other creditors because the proceeds of the sale benefited only one creditor (the bank).[40] Thus, the reasoning of the Supreme Court in this case does not shed direct light on the treatment of guarantees in this context.

Payments made in accordance with a legal obligation to make such a payment are generally much harder to avoid by a bankruptcy administrator.[41] Article 47 Fw is written for avoidance of legal acts that were required by a preexisting legal duty, such as payment of a due debt. Such a payment can be avoided only in two categories of cases: (i) cases in

---

39 *See* Dutch Supreme Court May 22, 1992, NJ 1992, 526 (Bosselaar q.q./Interniber—also known as Montana I); this is in line with later case law of the Supreme Court on prejudice to creditors, giving a broad interpretation of prejudice: Dutch Supreme Court October 19, 2001, ECLI:NL:HR:2001:ZC3654, NJ 2001, 654 (Diepstraten/Gilhuis q.q.); Dutch Supreme Court July 8, 2005, NJ 2005, 457, JOR 2005/230 (Van Dooren q.q./ABN AMRO II). *See also* R.J. Abendroth, "Herfinanciering van de Onderneming," *in* G. van Solinge e.a., De financiering van de onderneming, Voordrachten en discussieverslag van het gelijknamige congres op 11 en 12 november te Nijmegen, Serie vanwege het Van der Heijden Instituut deel 88, Deventer, Kluwer 2006, pp. 58-59.

40 Dutch Supreme Court July 8, 2005, NJ 2005, 457, JOR 2005/230 (Van Dooren q.q./ABN AMRO II).

41 Professional creditors use this system by ex ante making sure, through their general terms and conditions, that giving in to any request they may want to make in difficult times of their debtor can be qualified as a "due payment." The creditor can thus, also when in bad faith, request the debtor to post additional security, which is "due" on the basis of the general terms and conditions. If the bankruptcy administrator wants to avoid the posting of additional collateral, he will have to invoke Art. 47 Fw, not Art. 42 Fw.

which the party that received payment knew that a request for bankruptcy of the principal debtor had already been filed in court, and (ii) cases of conspiracy between principal debtor and creditor to prejudice other creditors (Art. 47 Fw).

It is important to note that especially professional financial creditors are able to (and do) manipulate the distinction that Dutch law makes between obligatory and voluntary legal acts. If there was a preexisting duty to perform the act, the act is considered obligatory. The courts have interpreted obligatory legal acts very broadly. If, for example, a contract allows a counterparty under certain circumstances to ask for additional security or for repayment of the full loan, consequent granting of security or repayment, respectively, is considered to have been obligatory, and thus largely immune from attacks based on transaction avoidance law. The standard terms that all major banks in the Netherlands use therefore contain a provision that the debtor has to post additional collateral when the bank reasonably requests so. Thus, such additional collateral, even if posted on the eve of bankruptcy and even if both debtor and creditor knew very well that bankruptcy of the debtor was soon to be expected, is probably immune from transaction avoidance attacks.

As already stated, an obligatory legal act can be avoided only in two categories of cases: (i) cases in which the party that received payment knew that a request for bankruptcy of the principal debtor had already been filed in court and (ii) cases of conspiracy between principal debtor and creditor to prejudice other creditors (Art. 47 Fw). The first category applies only to a very small number of cases and will, even if applicable, often be hard to prove for a bankruptcy administrator, unless the creditor himself filed for insolvency of the principal debtor before receiving the obligatory payment.

The Dutch Supreme Court has, furthermore, developed a rather narrow interpretation of "conspiracy" as referred to in Article 47 Fw. The landmark cases on this point are Gispen q.q./IFN[42] and Cikam/Simon q.q.[43] In Gispen q.q./IFN, the Dutch Supreme Court considered that conspiracy as referred to in Article 47 Fw should be understood to mean that both parties have intentionally and willingly prejudiced the other creditors of the principal debtor by paying this particular creditor. In the case itself, the Dutch Supreme Court considered such intention not to be present on the side of the principal debtor, because he gave in to pressure from the creditor to make the payment, and thus did not have the intention to prejudice other creditors. In Cikam/Simon q.q., the Dutch Supreme Court confirmed the judgment of the Court of Appeal and also specifically the consideration of that court that conspiracy as referred to in Article 47 Fw could be presumed to be present under the circumstances of the case. Those circumstances were, simply put, that Cikam GmbH made a due payment to sister company Cikam B.V., while the financial situation of Cikam GmbH was very troublesome, and while Cikam B.V.

42 Dutch Supreme Court March 24, 1995, *NJ* 1995, 628 (Gispen q.q./IFN); *See also* Dutch Supreme Court November 20, 1998, «*JOR*», 1999/19, m.nt. NEDF (Verkerk/Tiethoff q.q.).

43 Dutch Supreme Court March 7, 2003, *NJ* 2003, 429 (Cikam/Siemon q.q.).

knew this as well, given the fact that the management of that company was in the same hands.

In the case of a due payment on a guaranteed debt, the conspiracy that has to be shown by the bankruptcy administrator in order to rely on Article 47 Fw is a conspiracy between creditor and principal debtor, not between guarantor and principal debtor. Even if such conspiracy between creditor and principal debtor can be shown, avoidance on the basis of Article 47 Fw, like avoidance on the basis of Article 42 Fw, allows only for retrieving the sum from the creditor, not from the guarantor that profited indirectly. The question then is whether the fact that the guarantor, through direct or indirect influence on the principal debtor, indirectly favored himself by the payment of the principal debtor to the creditor, is a relevant circumstance in order to come to a presumption that there was a conspiracy between *creditor* and principal debtor. The *Cikam* case[44] cannot be applied directly, not even in the case that the guarantor and principal debtor are group companies in the same hands, because there is no direct payment to a group company, just indirect profit. The answer to this important question thus remains open.

In a district court judgment, the court has found that a guarantee relationship was a relevant circumstance to decide that creditor and principal debtor had conspired. The case was, however, very specific. Creditor and guarantor (who was the director and indirect shareholder of the principal debtor) had discussed the difficult situation of the principal debtor, which led to granting the creditor additional security (which was due) in exchange for canceling the guarantee for the same amount.[45] Here, we see a clear case of conspiracy, with the principal debtor (as represented by the guarantor) and the creditor at the table, contriving how to enrich the guarantor and the creditor at the expense of other creditors of the principal debtor.[46] However, Faber claims in a case note that the reasoning of the district court, in which the district court derives the intention of the principal debtor to prejudice the guaranteed creditor above other creditors from the fact that the director bargained for a benefit for himself (partly cancelation of the guarantee relationship), is slightly blunt. That is not convincing. The fact that the director of the principal debtor bargained for a benefit for himself as guarantor, clearly gives the director, and thus the company, incentive to prejudice the guaranteed creditor above other creditors. If the principal debtor then, and only after the benefit for the director

44 Dutch Supreme Court March 7, 2003, *NJ* 2003, 429 (Cikam/Siemon q.q.).

45 Of course, if the guarantor guaranteed the full debt of the creditor, such canceling would practically not have any effect, because giving the creditor additional security would already have benefited the guarantor. However, in this case, as often happens, the guarantor had only partly guaranteed the debt of the creditor. As a result, the additional security given to the creditor may not have benefited him if the remainder of the claim after foreclosing on security rights would still have exceeded the maximum amount of the guarantee. To make sure the guarantor did benefit from the transaction, the arrangement was made that part of the guarantee relationship was canceled.

46 *See also* on the case: De Weijs, 2010, pp. 160-165; N.E.D. Faber seems to have a differing opinion in his comment to the case: Utrecht District Court June 6, 2007, *JOR* 2008, 19, m.nt. Faber (Aerts q.q./Rabobank and FGH).

was bargained for, posts additional security to the guaranteed creditor, there should be enough evidence to conclude that conspiracy between principal debtor and guaranteed creditor has taken place.

More relevant is, however, how far this reasoning can be stretched. In the case discussed, the guarantor could profit only if the creditor canceled part of the guarantee, because the unsecured part of the claim of the guaranteed creditor was higher than the maximum of the guarantee. Thus, posting some additional security by the principal debtor would not as such have benefited the guarantor. Some bargaining, and thus a clear conspiracy, was necessary to this end. A situation could, however, also occur, and does often occur, in which posting additional security by the principal debtor will benefit the guarantor because his exposure is reduced, without having to bargain for such a benefit. In that situation, there is a clear incentive for the guarantor to influence the principal debtor to post additional security, to secure the benefit for the guarantor. If this guarantor is an insider, such as a director, a shareholder, or a group company, this incentive can arguably be attributed to the principal debtor. Whether this as such suffices to establish conspiracy between principal debtor and guaranteed creditor, however, remains unclear. Dutch law is underdeveloped on such cases.

It could be inferred from the Bosselaar q.q./Interniber case of the Dutch Supreme Court[47] that there is some attention to the indirect benefit the guarantor can have through a guarantee relationship. However, this case, first of all, concerned another question (whether the sale of caravans to the shareholder for a fair price indirectly prejudiced other creditors), and, secondly, the guarantee relationship was, as already discussed, probably not essential in the reasoning of the Supreme Court that there was prejudice. In that sense, not much weight can be attached to this case in answering the question of whether a guarantee relationship can lead to a presumption of conspiracy in the sense of Article 47 Fw.

The problem with acknowledging that an insider guarantor can enrich himself (and the guaranteed creditor) at the expense of nonguaranteed creditors and that the principal debtor therefore has incentive to disadvantage nonguaranteed creditors is that this may lead to counterintuitive results for guaranteed creditors. The guarantee can then be used as a circumstance in a case on transaction avoidance of a payment of a due debt to that creditor. Thus, the guarantee could arguably lead to less security, instead of more.[48] However, such reasoning paints a distorted picture. It should not be forgotten that the guarantee was, probably, the reason that the payment was made. In that sense, the existence of the guarantee relationship made the incentive for the selective payment arise in the first place. Moreover, if this was not the case and other, nonguaranteed creditors also received due payments around the same time, the payment could be regarded as a normal and not suspect payment, which would make the case for conspiracy weak. Lastly, it should be

47 Dutch Supreme Court May 22, 1992, NJ 1992, 526 (Bosselaar q.q./Interniber—also known as Montana I).
48 *See also* De Weijs, 2010, pp. 160-165.

kept in mind that transaction avoidance only annuls the payment to the creditor, not the guarantee itself. After having reimbursed the insolvency trustee, the creditor can possibly call upon the guarantor under the guarantee relationship. In that sense, the creditor is not worse off. Of course, the creditor is still worse off if the guarantor is insolvent as well, but in such a case the guarantee did not really represent any value other than leverage over the guarantor.[49] Whether annulment of the payment indeed brings the guarantee back to life is, however, somewhat unsure, because the Dutch doctrine in principle recognizes only *relative effect* of the annulment. This relative effect means the annulment, in principle, has effect only as between the bankruptcy administrator and the counterparty of the payment.

The lack of attention to the problem that the guarantor is incentivized by the guarantee to prefer the guaranteed creditor (and thus indirectly himself as guarantor by limiting his exposure under the guarantee) is remarkable given the fact that the courts do seem sensitive to the potency of the guarantee relationship in influencing the decision making of the guarantor in another context. In the case *Leliveld/Rabobank*, the guarantor himself had argued that pressure exerted by the bank through (inter alia) the guarantee made him act in ways that were ultimately detrimental to his own interests, which argument has been followed by the court.[50] It is, however, much more likely that the guarantee makes the guarantor act in his own interest rather than the exceptional cases in which such pressure makes the guarantor act in a manner detrimental to his own interests. In that sense, it is all the more remarkable that the courts have little attention to this mechanism in the context of preference law.

Lastly, it should be noted that Article 47 Fw applies only to legal acts. Wealth transfers can remain covert, especially in cases where the wealth transfer is not a payment but another fact pattern that prefers the guaranteed creditor, such as a delayed bankruptcy filing or accelerated processing of raw materials. Because Article 47 Fw applies only to a legal act (*rechtshandeling*), such covert wealth transfers escape the (very limited) scrutiny of Dutch preference law in any case.

In short, Dutch transaction avoidance law fails to deal with indirect preferences. Dutch law distinguishes between avoidance of obligatory and voluntary acts. This distinction is somewhat flawed in the sense that it allows creditors to contract around it by ex ante making sure, using contractual provisions, that preferences given on the eve of bankruptcy will be qualified as obligatory payments. Avoidance of obligatory payments is generally difficult under Dutch law, and the circumstance that an insider such as a manager or shareholder has guaranteed the debt that was paid may arguably make avoidance of the payment easier, but what is very unclear is whether this is indeed the case and if it is, how much easier. Furthermore, in the case of both obligatory and voluntary payments,

49 J.L. Westbrook, "Two Thoughts About Insider Preferences," *Minnesota Law Review*, Vol. 76, 1991, pp. 73-98.

50 Court of Appeal Arnhem-Leeuwarden March 27, 2018, ECLI:NL:GHARL:2018:2893 (*Leliveld / Rabobank*).

Dutch law strongly relies on subjective factors that are often hard to prove. Relevant objective factors, such as the fact that an insider has indirectly profited from a certain transaction, hardly play a role, either in the statutory law or in the case law.

5.2 *Shareholder Liability for Unlawful Indirect Benefits through Guarantees*

A shareholder that has received an indirect benefit through a guarantee could act unlawfully (Art. 6:162 BW) in his role in creating such benefits, even when the payment or other act of the debtor that has created the benefit cannot be avoided by relying on transaction avoidance law. We can roughly distinguish between two types of unlawful shareholder behavior toward creditors.[51] The first category concerns liability because of unlawful distributions to shareholders, the second concerns unjustifiably continuing the company in difficult times. The first category is particularly relevant in the context of indirect preferences given through guarantees. When payments on company debts guaranteed by shareholders are made, the shareholder limits his exposure and thus indirectly receives a distribution. Payments on shareholder-guaranteed debts can thus be seen as covert distributions.

The Dutch Supreme Court has, in some exceptional cases, held that such behavior can indeed be unlawful toward creditors. In the *Keulen/Bouwfonds* case, Bouwfonds was in control of another entity (a nonprofit entity, a "Stichting" (foundation)) but withdrew and foreclosed on a loan when it heard that the local government would not finance the entity and quickly made sure its claim on the entity was fully satisfied.[52] The foundation had to liquidate, and all the creditors were paid only 65%. Keulen, one of the creditors, pursued Bouwfonds for its allegedly unlawful behavior. The Supreme Court held that the behavior of Bouwfonds could indeed be unlawful if it, when receiving the payment, should have seriously taken the possibility of a shortfall after liquidation into account. However, the Court of Appeal had already held that it was not sufficiently proven that Bouwfonds had an indication of such a shortfall.[53] The case shows that although establishing liability of a shareholder (or otherwise controlling entity) that seemingly favored himself as a creditor above other creditors is not easy on the basis of an unlawful act, a stricter norm applies to the liability of such a shareholder/creditor than to other normal creditors. Whereas a normal creditor will typically not act unlawfully when he receives payment in the vicinity of insolvency, not even if he knew of the financially deplorable

---

51 *See* for this distinction: Asser/Maeijer, Van Solinge & Nieuwe Weme 2-II* 2009, no. 842-843.

52 The relationship between Bouwfonds and the Stichting (foundation) can be seen as analogous to a parent-subsidiary relationship, *see* case note Van der Grinten to Dutch Supreme Court May 9, 1986, *NJ* 1986, 792 (Keulen/Bouwfonds).

53 Dutch Supreme Court May 9, 1986, *NJ* 1986, 792 (Keulen/Bouwfonds). *See* on the case Van Schilfgaarde, 1987, p. 84.

state of his debtor, the shareholder/creditor could act unlawfully if it can be proven that he knew of serious financial difficulties.[54]

Another case that deserves attention in this context is *Nimox*.[55] Nimox sold its claim, which was essentially a dividend payment turned into a loan, on its full subsidiary Auditrade to a third party that paid Nimox for the claim. That third party had an abundance of security rights, and could thus rank above other creditors, also for the claim bought from Nimox, in the bankruptcy of Auditrade that soon followed. Such behavior, essentially consisting of executing a decision to pay out dividend on a moment that this is clearly not justified and enforcing this dividend payment through a creative construction, can be unlawful according to the Supreme Court.[56]

Both in *Nimox* and in *Keulen/Bouwfonds*, the benefits received by the shareholder either directly or de facto amounted to withdrawals of share capital.[57] The accusation to the shareholder in such a case is that he pushes the corporation into a state of undercapitalization, which can be unlawful.[58] Payments that simply benefit a shareholder as an insider can arguably be distinguished from such withdrawals de facto of share capital, though of course dependent on what qualifies as de facto share capital.[59] Under current Dutch law, payments on third-party loans that are guaranteed by shareholders, in general probably do not qualify as withdrawals of share capital. Rather, as Barneveld also argues, such payments can be seen under the current law as, possibly, being in conflict with the paritas creditorum (Section 3:277 BW).

A good example of such a case is *Coral/Stalt*, in which the Supreme Court held, simply put, that a parent company is not free to favor itself as a creditor above other creditors after deciding to stop the activities of a subsidiary, except in special circumstances.[60] Two remarks should be made here. Firstly, the facts in the *Coral/Stalt* case present a rather extreme example, in which the decision to discontinue the business was already made before the payments to the shareholders were made. In other words, the payments were clearly part of a de facto liquidation of the business. The question remains whether a shareholder can already be held liable for the damage done by such payments in the period before the decision to discontinue.[61] Secondly, in *Coral/Stalt*, the debtor company directly favored the shareholder. The question remains whether the rule can be applied to the situation in which the debtor company pays an unrelated third-party creditor, for

54 Case note Van der Grinten to Dutch Supreme Court May 9, 1986, *NJ* 1986, 792 (Keulen/Bouwfonds).

55 Dutch Supreme Court November 8, 1991, *NJ* 1992, 174 (*Nimox/Van den End q.q.*).

56 Para. 3.3.1 of Dutch Supreme Court November 8, 1991, *NJ* 1992, 174 (*Nimox/Van den End q.q.*).

57 Compare Barneveld, 2014, pp. 481, 493.

58 Barneveld, 2014, pp. 481, 491.

59 *See* Barneveld, 2014, p. 495; of course, whether such a distinction can be made simply depends on the qualification of what is (de facto) seen as share capital. If an insider guarantee is qualified as share capital, limiting exposure under the guarantee is a withdrawal of share capital.

60 Dutch Supreme Court June 12, 1998, *NJ* 1998, 727 (Coral/Stalt); Barneveld, 2014, pp. 495-496.

61 *See also* Barneveld, 2014, pp. 495-496, who assumes this to be the case insofar as the involved actors understood or should have understood that bankruptcy was imminent.

which the shareholder acts as guarantor. The shareholder does not directly receive a payment in this case, but indirectly limits his exposure.

The facts in the *Sobi/Hurks* case show that guarantees can lead to preferential payments, but the Supreme Court does not seem to acknowledge this, or at least not explicitly.[62] The Court of Appeal had established that the shareholder should, from a certain date onward, have understood that new creditors would be prejudiced and held the shareholder liable for the debts of those new creditors (and did not hold the shareholders liable on the theory of unlawful distributions to shareholders). What happened after that date (but possibly also partly before) is that the principal debtor paid off debts with the bank, which the shareholder had guaranteed. The guarantee relationship can explain the behavior of the shareholder.[63] It could be that the shareholder fully understood that the subsidiary was not a viable company anymore, and that new creditors would from a certain moment on be prejudiced, but still kept this quiet and opportunistically waited with filing for insolvency in order to use the future incoming payments to limit its own exposure under the guarantee. Neither the Supreme Court nor the Court of Appeal seems to have fully acknowledged the guarantee as a relevant circumstance.[64] Moreover, if they had acknowledged this fact, it should have led to liability of the shareholder not only toward the new creditors, but also toward old creditors because they are also prejudiced by such indirect distributions to shareholders.[65]

As becomes apparent from the cases discussed, the Supreme Court has in some rather exceptional circumstances found unlawful behavior of a shareholder by favoring himself as a creditor present, while it also becomes apparent from the exceptional nature of these cases that such unlawful behavior is far from easy to show for another creditor or bankruptcy administrator. Concerning a shareholder that indirectly profits from payments made on a loan guaranteed by him, the creditor prejudiced by this will at least have to show that the shareholder should have seriously taken bankruptcy, and the possibility of a shortfall in that bankruptcy, of the company into account at the moment of receiving the indirect benefit. However, as case law on such indirect benefits in this context is currently absent, even that may not prove sufficient. The objective fact that a guarantee by a shareholder plays an important role in the dynamics is not recognized as such.

5.3 *Director Liability for Insider Preferences*

An important deterrent force on insider dealing with guarantees in the context of business finance may come from director liability rules for such behavior. Roughly two situa-

62 De Weijs, 2010, p. 163.
63 *Id.*
64 *Id.*
65 *Id.*

tions should be distinguished in this context: (a) payment of the guaranteed debt has just prejudiced other creditors and (b) payment of the guaranteed debt has both prejudiced creditors and damaged the company. The latter situation really is the exception and is mostly of theoretical interest. Payments to creditors normally do not damage the debtor itself. This category is therefore left out of the discussion. The distinction is relevant in light of director liability, because, under Dutch law, the rules on director liability toward the shareholders and/or the company differ from the rules on director liability toward outsiders such as creditors.

Creditors of the company and bankruptcy administrators can pursue directors of the company for unlawful behavior in the case that serious blame can be attributed to a director because he or she has effectuated, or allowed, that the company does not live up to its statutory or contractual obligations, while the director should have understood that the behavior of the company that he or she has allowed or effectuated would result in a failure to meet its obligations and that the company would also not provide sufficient opportunity for recovery.[66] In the case of unlawful behavior that falls in this category, generally both the individual creditors and the insolvency administrator (on behalf of the joint insolvency creditors) could bring a claim against the director for such unlawful behavior.[67]

This category of debtor liability can be relevant in the context of payments on debts guaranteed by shareholders and/or directors of the debtor, although the relevance of such guarantees to the application is rather unsure. Generally, directors are free to choose whom to pay first, but this can change near insolvency. If the directors are aware of the serious financial difficulties of a company and that a certain payment will prejudice the other creditors, they would be acting unlawfully if they made the payment anyway.[68] It is clear that directors who (can) foresee that insolvency is unavoidable are not allowed to make selective payments to creditors anymore and will be liable for the damage done to creditors if they represent the company in making such payments anyway. Somewhat unclear in the doctrine is whether selective payments made to insiders, such as shareholders, group companies, or the directors themselves, can be unlawful already before selective payments to outsiders would be unlawful. This indeed follows from both the

66 Dutch Supreme Court December 8, 2006, *NJ* 2006, 659, ECLI:NL:HR:2006:AZ0758 (Ontvanger/Roelofsen); the Supreme Court has also recognized another category of unlawful behavior of directors toward creditors, but this other type is generally not relevant to cases of selective payment. This type concerns directors to which serious blame can be attributed because of representing the company in contracting with third parties, while they knew or should have known that the company would not be able to perform and would also not provide sufficient opportunity for recovery (Dutch Supreme Court October 6, 1989, NJ 1990, 286 (Beklamel)).

67 Dutch Supreme Court January 14, 1983, *NJ* 1983, 597 (Peeters q.q./Gatzen); Dutch Supreme Court December 21, 2001, *NJ* 2005, 95 (Lunderstadt/De Kok c.s.).

68 Dutch Supreme Court December 8, 2006, *NJ* 2006, 659, ECLI:NL:HR:2006:AZ0758 (Ontvanger/Roelofsen); Den Bosch Court of Appeal, January 19, 2010, *JOR* 2010/113 (Stoets Holding/Bohncke); Arnhem Court of Appeal, September 15, 2009, *JOR* 2010/112 (Beijer/Willems q.q.).

Beijer/Willems q.q. case of the Arnhem Court of Appeal and the *Stoets/Bohncke* case of the Den Bosch Court of Appeal.[69] In the latter case, the Court of Appeal explained that even though selective payments to creditors are generally allowed even in difficult times, the circumstances of the case, such as the fact that only insiders were paid, can lead to the conclusion that the directors have acted unlawfully.[70]

However, that still leaves the question on indirect payments to insiders somewhat open. A payment on a loan guaranteed by an insider is not a direct payment to an insider, but an insider indirectly profits. This circumstance arguably makes qualification of a selective payment in difficult times as unlawful more likely, but Dutch law is unclear and underdeveloped on this point. Moreover, even if such selective payments are unlawful because of the moment at which they were made in combination with the fact that an insider profited, there is, in the current doctrine, possibly still room for justification.[71] Such a justification could arguably be more likely to be accepted by a court in cases of payments that only indirectly benefited insiders than in cases of direct selective payments to insider creditors.[72]

A judgment of the Amsterdam Court of Appeal (*Pieper/Mentzel c.s.*) illustrates that point well.[73] The accusation had been made toward the director that the available funds (more than 1 million Euro) had been almost exclusively used to pay off debts for which the director was personally liable toward those creditors. The payments had thus limited the exposure of the director under that contractual liability. The Court of Appeal first reiterates that a director should, also in the case of distress and when it is clear that not all creditors will receive full satisfaction from the available funds, have the freedom to pay those creditors on which the company is most dependent regarding the continuance of the business. The Court of Appeal acknowledges that if the director has indeed adjusted payments of the company to suit his personal interests of being released from a personal guarantee, the conclusion should usually be reached that the director has improperly managed the company. However, the court also directly relativizes this statement, by stating that the simple fact that a personal interest of a director is served by a certain payment does not mean that the director cannot justifiably make the assessment that the continuance of the company is coincidently also best served by that payment, which should thus also be made. In the case itself, the director had argued that the payments

---

69 Arnhem Court of Appeal, September 15, 2009, *JOR* 2010/112 (Beijer/Willems q.q.). Den Bosch Court of Appeal, 19 January 2010, *JOR* 2010/113 (Stoets Holding/Bohncke). In her case comment to the cases, Rijckenberg argues against such a distinction between payments to insiders and payments to outsiders, but instead argues that this distinction could have some influence on the question of whether the payment, if made after a point that directors should have understood that insolvency was very near, could be justified or not.

70 Den Bosch Court of Appeal, January 19, 2010, *JOR* 2010/113 (Stoets Holding/Bohncke), para. 8.6.1.

71 Dutch Supreme Court June 12, 1998, *NJ* 1998, 727 (Coral/Stalt).

72 Compare case note Rijckenberg, para. 13, Arnhem Court of Appeal, September 15, 2009, *JOR* 2010/112 (Beijer/Willems q.q).

73 Amsterdam Court of Appeal, ECLI:NL:GHAMS:2012:BW1995 (*Pieper/Mentzel c.s.*), r.o. 3.32.

were indeed in the interest of the company, and the Court of Appeal accepted this fact as not contested.

Although the Court of Appeal is not entirely clear on this, we could infer that the fact that certain payments have served the personal interests of a director because of a guarantee relationship with the creditor can help the claimant somewhat in proving that the director has behaved improperly, but not sure is how much this can help. The claimant should show that (1) the payment was made at a time in which the director should have understood that not all creditors would receive full satisfaction from the available funds and that (2) the director had a personal interest in such payments. It is then for the director to show that, although such personal interest existed, the payments were essential from a going concern point of view. If such a personal interest of the director would have been absent, the claimant would possibly also have to show that the payment was not strictly necessary, as the starting point of the Court of Appeal was that the director should be given the freedom to decide which payments are necessary. In other words, the existence of a personal interest of the director, here based on a guarantee, puts the burden of proof that the payment was indeed necessary from a going concern point of view on the director, whereas absent a guarantee the burden to show that the payment was not necessary from a going concern point of view lies with the claimant.

The question of liability of directors for preferring one creditor above another is particularly also relevant in the context where no payment was made but in which factual behavior of the debtor has preferred a certain guaranteed creditor (and indirectly thus the insider guarantor) above other creditors. Think of the example of continuing the business, or even speeding up the business, such as the processing of raw materials into a finished product, by which a certain creditor (automatically) gets a security right. Articles 42 and 47 Fw only apply to legal acts and are thus unable to police such behavior. The fact that Articles 42 and 47 Fw do not regulate such behavior does not compromise the possibility of a claim based on an unlawful act (Section 6:162 BW) on a director.[74]

6 RECOMMENDATIONS

This report has shown that Dutch law has little attention to the opaque dynamics that a group structure perforated by guarantees can create. Not only does Dutch law have little attention to piercing guarantees when considering veil-piercing cases, but it also fully allows double proofing of claims and hardly puts any brakes on preferential payments on guaranteed loans on the eve of bankruptcy. Three general recommendations are put forward to regulate the adverse dynamics created by perforated group structures:

74 *See also* R. van den Sigtenhorst & B. Winters, "Bestuurdersaansprakelijkheid wegens benadeling van Schuldeisers En de Samenhang Met Pauliana," *in* Van Bekkum, Kreileman, Schuijling & Van Solinge, *Aansprakelijkheid van Bestuurders en Commissarissen*, Deventer, Kluwer, 2017, para. 15.4.4.

- Clearly recognize guarantees that pierce group structures as an important factor in decisions on veil piercing and substantive consolidation.
- Limit double proofing of claims through guarantees in the context of corporate groups.
- Limit the incentive for making preferential payments on guaranteed loans by:
  1. making avoidance of such preferential payments easier (after which the guaranteed creditor should be allowed recourse on the guarantor(s));
  2. making a direct claim by the bankruptcy administrator on the guarantor possible; and
  3. consider indirect profit to an insider guarantor (such as a group company) as an important factor in shareholder and director liability cases concerning damages because of preferential payments.

Printed by Libri Plureos GmbH in Hamburg,
Germany

9 789462 369573